BRANCH LINES TO ALTON

Vic Mitchell and Keith Smith

First published 1984
Reprinted 1985

ISBN 0 906520 11 8

© *Middleton Press, 1984*

Phototypeset by   CitySet Ltd, Chichester

Published by   Middleton Press
Easebourne Lane
Midhurst, West Sussex
GU29 9AZ

Printed and bound by   Biddles Ltd
Guildford and King's Lynn

INDEX TO SECTIONS

INDEX TO STATIONS

ACKNOWLEDGEMENTS

Our sincere thanks go to those mentioned in the credits to the captions and also to J. Adams, C. Hayward, Mid-Hants Railway Preservation Society Ltd., R. Randall, K. Robertson, Mrs. E. Wallis and D. Wallis. We are grateful for the help received from D. Dornom, M. Grainger and D. Mercer in the darkroom; Mrs. E. Fisk and N. Stanyon in proof reading, and our wives in so many other ways.

MAPS

Except where otherwise stated, the scale is 25" to 1 mile but the following initial letters apply throughout.

BM	Bench Mark
Cr	Crane
MP	Mile Post
SB	Signal Box
SP	Signal Post

GEOGRAPHICAL SETTING

The unnamed chalk mass linking the North Downs, to the West of Farnham, with the South Downs, in the Petersfield area, is crossed by all three lines featured in this album.

The line from Basingstoke traversed the chalk uplands for almost its entire length, mainly around the 500ft. contour.

The line from Fareham entered the Meon Valley after crossing two miles of difficult clay and sand of the Reading Beds which necessitated problematical tunnelling, described elsewhere in this album. After crossing the eastward turn of the valley on a viaduct near West Meon, the line passed through West Meon tunnel and reached its summit (519ft above sea level) after leaving Privett tunnel.

The route from Winchester was up the valley of the River Itchen (whose mouth is at Southampton) almost to Alresford. After a brief glimpse of the River Arle it climbed "over the Alps", in the words of local train crews, with the summit at Medstead.

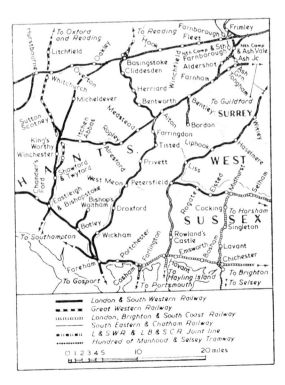

(Railway Magazine).

HISTORICAL BACKGROUND

By 1840 the infant London and South Western Railway completed its main line from London to Southampton and in 1841 built a branch from Eastleigh (then known as Bishopstoke) to Gosport, via Fareham to serve the Portsmouth area. Prior to the opening of the branch on 29th November, the tunnel north of Fareham caved in and so a short cutting was created between the two remaining parts of the tunnel. Four days after the opening of the line, the new cutting filled in with an almost uncontrollable semi-liquid clay and train services were suspended until 7th February 1842.

In 1852 a LSWR line reached Alton, via Farnham. Nine years later the Alton, Alresford and Winchester Railway Company was empowered to extend the route westwards and this was opened to traffic on 2nd October 1865, trains being operated by the LSWR on behalf of the local company, by then known as the Mid Hants Railway Company. Inter-mediate stations were provided at Ropley, Alresford and Itchen Abbas. Three years later a station was opened at Medstead.

The Mid Hants line was always regarded as a secondary route and after electrification between London and Alton in 1937 it was run very much as a branch line, with steam operated push-pull trains providing the majority of the connecting services until the introduction of diesel-electric multiple units (DEMUs) in 1957.

During the 1965-67 period many weekend trains between London and Bournemouth were diverted via Alton whilst the main line was being electrified. Shortly after this, the first proposal for closure was made which led to a fierce local opposition campaign being launched. This lasted over five years and ended when the last trains ran on 4th February 1973, despite plans for electrification being announced in 1970.

Two groups set about reviving the line but

were described by the Railway Magazine as *competing with themselves over the corpse*. Despite numerous difficulties and recourse to the Ombudsman, trains started running again between Alresford and Ropley on 30th April 1977. With massive volunteer effort and considerable professional skill the track was relaid to Medstead to allow services to be extended there on 28th May 1983.

At the time of writing, work has started on relaying the route to Alton to provide connection with British Rail.

In the last decade of the 19th century the Great Western Railway was considering building a line to Portsmouth. Whilst its admirers considered GWR to stand for *God's Wonderful Railway* its critics regarded them as meaning *Great Way Round*. The latter observation would have certainly applied to a journey from Paddington to Portsmouth. Contemporary railway politics being what they were, the LSWR counter-proposed a light railway to link Basingstoke and Alton. This is thought to be the first railway to be built under the Light Railways Act of 1896, which permitted simpler safety measures (e.g. level crossing gates were not required), subject to severe overall speed limits.

The first sod was cut on 22nd July 1898, near Basingstoke, and the line opened throughout on 1st June 1901, without any ceremony. It joined the Mid Hants line at Butts Junction where the single track timber bridge was replaced by a double track girder structure. The railway continued uneventfully until closed on 30th Decemebr 1916, after which most of the permanent way was lifted for re-use by the Army in France. The closure also helped to overcome a staff shortage on the LSWR caused by WWI. The company provided a lorry to carry the local agricultural traffic.

1956

Table 47 LONDON, ALTON, ALRESFORD, EASTLEIGH and SOUTHAMPTON

Miles	Down	Week Days													Sundays			
		am	am Mondays to Fridays	am Saturdays only	am	pm Mondays to Fridays	pm Saturdays only	pm	pm	pm	pm Mondays to Fridays	pm Saturdays only	pm	pm Mondays to Fridays	am	am	pm	pm
	LONDON Waterloo 70 .. dep	6 25	725	7 28	10f27	1257	1 2	2f27	3f27	4K27	5 57	5 57	657	7 57	7 25	1027	327	6 57
—	**Alton** .... dep	**7 53**	**855**	**9 20**	**12 5**	**2 30**	**2 30**	**4 10**	**5 5**	**6 2**	**7 25**	**7 30**	**840**	**9 35**	**8 55**	**12 5**	**455**	**8 20**
51¼	Medstead and Four Marks	8 5	9 7	9 32	12 17	2 42	2 42	4 22	5 17	6 14	7 37	7 42	852	9 47	9 7	1217	5 7	8 32
54¼	Ropley	8 11	912	9 38	12 23	2 48	2 48	4 28	5 23	6 19	7 43	7 47	858	9 53	9 12	1222	512	8 38
57	Alresford	8C18	917	9 43	12 29	2 54	2J58	4C34	5B39	6C25	7G52	7C54	9 2	9 57	9 17	1227	517	8 43
60½	Itchen Abbas	8 24	923	9 49	12 33	3 0	3 4	4 40	5 45	6 31	7 58	8 0	9 8	10 3	9 23	1233	523	8 50
65¾	Winchester City .. .. .. arr	8 35	937	10 1	12 44	3 13	3 16	4V51	5 56	6 42	8 10	8 12	919	1014	9 33	1244	534	9 2
69	28 Shawford .... arr	8 42	943	10 7	12 50	3 19	3 22	4V57	6 2	..	8 15	8 17	926	..	9 39	1250	.	9 8
72¾	28 Eastleigh .. .. „	8 50	950	1015	12 58	3 27	3 30	5V 3	6 9	....	8 23	8 25	934	....	9 47	1258	...	9 16
75	28 Swaythling .... „	..	.	..	..	..	..	5 13	..	..	..	..	.	..	9b58	..	.	9 23
76½	28 St. Denys .. .. „	....	...	....	....	....	....	5 17	....	....	....	....	...	....	10b 2	....	...	9 27
77½	28 Northam .... „	..	.	..	..	..	..	5 21	..	..	..	..	.	..	..	..	.	..
78¼	28 **Southampton Terminus.** „	....	...	....	....	....	....	**5 24**	....	....	....	....	...	....	**10b 8**	....	...	**9 33**

Miles	Up	Week Days														Sundays			
		am	am	am Mons. to Fris.	am Saturdays only	pm Saturdays only	pm Mondays toFridays	pm Mondays toFridays	pm Saturdays only	pm	pm	pm	pm Saturdays only	pm Mondays to Fridays	pm Mondays to Fridays	am	am	pm	pm
	28 **Southampton Terminus.** dep	..	..		..	..			.	..	..	**523**	**652**	**658**	**7 40**	..	..	..	..
¾	28 Northam .... „	....	....		....	....			....	....	....	526	655	7 1	7 43	....	....	....	....
1¾	28 St. Denys .. .. „	..	..		..	..			.	..	..	530	659	7 5	7 48	..	..	..	..
3¼	28 Swaythling .... „	....	....		....	....			....	....	....	534	7 3	7 9	7 51	....	....	....	....
5½	28 Eastleigh .. .. „	6 35	7 42	1016	1036	1 5	1 15	2 20	224	3 59	4 55	544	715	715	7 58	7 45	1046	3 42	..
9¼	28 Shawford .... „	6 42	7 49	1023	..	1 12	1 22	2 27	231	4 6	5 2	553	724	722	8 6	7 52	1053	3 49	....
12½	Winchester City .. .. .. dep	6 50	7 58	1032	1051	1 20	1 29	2 34	238	4 14	5 9	6 4	733	730	8 14	7 59	11 0	3 56	7 27
17¾	Itchen Abbas	7 2	8 10	1044	11 5	1 32	1 41	2 46	250	4 26	5 21	618	745	742	8 27	8 11	1112	4 8	7 38
21¼	Alresford	7 9	8 17	1051	1112	1 39	1 48	2C55	257	4C35	5 28	625	753	750	8 34	8 18	1119	4 15	7 45
24	Ropley	7 16	8 24	1058	1119	1 46	1 55	3 2	3 4	4 42	5 35	632	8 0	757	8 41	8 25	1126	4 22	7 53
27	Medstead and Four Marks	7 25	8 33	11 7	1128	1 55	2 4	3 11	312	4 51	5 44	640	8 9	8 6	8 50	8 34	1135	4 31	8 1
31½	**Alton** .... arr	**7 34**	**8 42**	**1116**	**1137**	**2 4**	**2 13**	**3 20**	**321**	**5 0**	**5 52**	**649**	**818**	**815**	**9 2**	**8 43**	**1144**	**4 41**	**8 10**
78¼	**LONDON Waterloo 70** .. arr	8 58	9L57	1246	1 17	3 45	3 46	4 46	445	6 46	7 16	816	946	946	10d46	1016	1 16	6 16	9H46

B Arr 5 27 pm
b Commences 1st July
C Arr 2 minutes *earlier*

d 10 41 pm on Tuesdays, Wednesdays and Thursdays 24th July to 23rd August
f 3 minutes later on Saturdays
G Arr 4 minutes *earlier*

H 9 40 pm 22nd July to 26th August
J Arr 5 minutes *earlier*
K Dep 4 47 pm Mondays to Fridays
L Arr 10 17 am on Saturdays
V 1 minute later on Saturdays

When the Southern Railway was formed in 1923 it decided not to reopen the line, as it had been losing about £4000 per annum before closure. Following strong local pressure, the SR reluctantly relaid the track but with no passing loops. It was re-opened, again without ceremony, on 18th August 1924 but no station masters were provided at the intermediate stations.

Eventually passenger services ceased on 12th September 1932 but freight services were maintained between Basingstoke and Bentworth until 30th May 1936. The extremities of the line (to Thorneycroft's factory and Treloar's Hospital) remained in occasional use up to 1967.

The Meon Valley line was authorised by an Act of Parliament dated 3rd June 1897. The LSWR was empowered to construct a single line railway but with all the civil engineering capable of receiving double track if required. This was never necessary but between Alton and Butts Junction the existing Mid Hants line was doubled and between Knowle Junction and Fareham a new line of double track was provided, which avoided the notorious tunnels mentioned earlier.

Train services commenced on 1st June 1903 on which day free single tickets to the next station were available – walk back or pay up! The few changes that occurred on the line, particularly at the junctions, are detailed in the relevant captions. The electrification of the services east of Alton in 1937 had a similar effect on the Meon Valley line as it did on the Mid Hants route – a down grading to virtual branch line status – hence the title of this album.

Closure to passengers came on 5th February 1955 along with withdrawal of freight

1948

LONDON, ALTON, DROXFORD, FAREHAM, EASTLEIGH, and SOUTHAMPTON

(1948 railway timetable: LONDON, ALTON, DROXFORD, FAREHAM, EASTLEIGH, and SOUTHAMPTON — Down and Up services, Week Days and Sundays)

Table 71   LONDON, ALTON, DROXFORD, FAREHAM, EASTLEIGH, and SOUTHAMPTON

Down

Miles		Week Days																				Sundays				
		a.m	a.m	a.m	a.m	a.m	a.m	p.m	p.m	p.m	p.m	p.m	p.m	p.m	p.m			a.m	a.m		p.m	p.m
	Waterloo 76 ..... dep	5 55	6 25	7 25	7 25	10 27	11 57	12 57	2 27	2 57	3 27	4 47	5 57	6 57				7 25	10 27		3 27	6 57
46½	Alton .... dep	7 35	..	..	9 5	..	1 30	4 30	..	4 37	..	..	..	..				..	..		..	..
50½	Farringdon	7 45	..	..	9 12	..	1 37	4 37	..	..	..	..	..	..				..	..		..	..
52½	Tisted	7 50	..	..	9 16	..	1 41	4 41	..	..	..	..	..	..				..	..		..	..
55½	Privett..............	7 57	..	..	9 24	..	1 49	4 48	..	..	..	..	..	..				..	..		..	..
59½	West Meon	8 5	..	..	9 31	..	1 56	4 56	..	..	..	..	..	..				..	..		..	..
63	Droxford B	8 15	..	..	9 39	..	2 4	5 3	..	..	..	..	..	..				..	..		..	..
65½	Wickham	8 27	..	..	9 48	..	2 12	5 12	..	..	..	..	..	..				..	..		..	..
70½	Knowle Halt	8 32	..	..	9 54	..	2 18	5 18	..	..	..	..	..	..				..	..		..	..
72½	Fareham .... arr	8 37	..	..	9 59	..	2 23	5 23	..	..	..	..	..	..				..	..		..	..
	Alton .... dep	..	7 53	8 55	..	12 5	..	2 30	4 10	..	5 5	5 27	5 38	..				9 0	12 5		4 55	4 20
51¼	Medstead & Four Marks	..	8 5	9 7	..	12 17	..	2 42	4 22	..	5 17	5 14	7 37	5 50				9 12	12 17		5 7	4 32
54½	Ropley..............	..	8 11	9 12	..	12 23	..	2 48	4 28	..	5 23	6 19	7 43	5 56				9 24	12 27		5 12	4 38
57	Alresford	..	8 18	9 17	..	12 27	..	2 54	4 34	..	5 39	6 25	7 54	6 1				9 30	12 33		5 17	4 41
60½	Itchen Abbas	..	8 24	9 23	..	12 33	..	3 0	4 40	..	5 45	6 31	8 0	6 7				9 41	12 44		5 23	4 50
64½	Winchester City B arr	..	8 35	9 35	..	12 44	..	3 13	4 51	..	5 56	6 42	8 12	6 19				9 47	12 50		5 34	9 2
69¾	74 Shawford D .... arr	..	8 42	9 41	..	12 50	..	3 19	4 57	..	6 2	..	8 17	4 25				9 55	12 58		5 40	9 8
73¾	74 Eastleigh F .... u	..	8 50	9 49	..	12 58	..	3 27	5 3	..	6 9	..	8 23	9 34				..	..		5 48	9 16
75¾	7.8 waythling....... u	..	..	..	..	..	..	..	5 13	..	..	..	5 17	..				..	..		5 54	9 23
77¼	7 St. Denys .... u	..	..	..	..	..	..	..	5 17	..	..	..	..	..				..	..		5 58	9 27
78¾	74 Northam .... u	..	..	..	..	..	..	..	5 21	..	..	..	..	..				..	..		6 2	..
79	74 Southampton G .. u	..	..	..	..	..	..	..	5 24	..	..	..	..	..				..	..		6 49	9 33

Up

Miles		Week Days																	Sundays		
		a.m	a.m	a.m	a.m	a.m	a.m	p.m	p.m	p.m	p.m	p.m	p.m	p.m	p.m			a.m	a.m	p.m	p.m
	74 Southampton G dep	..	..	..	..	..	..	..	..	..	5 23	..	6 58	..				..	..	..	..
¾	74 Northam .... u	..	..	..	..	..	..	..	..	..	5 26	..	7 1	..				..	..	..	..
1¾	74 St. Denys .... u	..	..	..	..	..	..	..	..	..	5 30	..	7 5	..				..	..	..	..
3¼	74 Swaythling ...... u	..	..	..	..	..	..	..	..	..	5 34	..	7 9	..				..	..	..	..
5¼	74 Eastleigh F ..... dep	6 35	7 42	..	1016	1016	..	1 15	2 20	..	3 59	4 55	5 44	..	7 15			7 45	1046	3 42	..
9½	74 Shawford D ..... dep	6 42	7 49	..	1023	1023	..	1 22	2 27	..	4 6	5 2	5 53	..	7 22			7 52	1053	3 49	..
12½	Winchester City B dep	6 50	7 58	..	1032	1032	..	1 24	2 34	..	4 14	5 9	6 4	..	7 32			7 59	11 0	3 56	7 31
15¼	Itchen Abbas ...... u	7 2	8 10	..	1044	1044	..	1 41	2 46	..	4 26	5 21	6 18	..	7 44			8 11	1112	4 8	7 42
2	Alresford .... u	7 9	8 17	..	1051	1051	..	1 48	2 53	..	4 33	5 28	6 25	..	7 52			8 20	1119	4 15	7 49
24¾	Ropley .... u	7 16	8 24	..	1058	1058	..	1 55	3 0	..	4 42	5 35	6 32	..	8 0			8 27	1126	4 22	7 56
27¾	Medstead & Four Marks	7 25	8 33	..	11 7	11 7	..	2 4	3 9	..	4 51	5 44	6 40	..	8 9			8 36	1135	4 32	8 5
31	Alton A .... arr	7 34	8 42	..	1116	1116	..	2 13	3 18	..	5 0	5 52	6 49	..	8 18			8 45	1144	4 41	8 14
—	Mls Fareham ...... dep	..	..	7 58	..	1156	..	2 43	..	..	..	6 48	..					..	..	..	..
—	2 Knowle Halt	..	..	8 2	..	12 0	..	2 53	..	..	..	6 58	..					..	..	..	..
—	4½ Wickham	..	..	8 7	..	12 5	..	2 58	..	..	..	6 58	..					..	..	..	..
—	7¼ Droxford B	..	..	8 17	..	1215	..	3 8	..	..	..	7 8	..					..	..	..	..
—	13¼ West Meon	..	..	8 25	..	1223	..	3 18	..	..	..	7 17	..					..	..	..	..
—	17 Privett...........	..	..	8 34	..	1232	..	3 29	..	..	..	7 27	..					..	..	..	..
—	20½ Tisted	..	..	8 40	..	1238	..	3 36	..	..	..	7 34	..					..	..	..	..
—	22½ Farring on	..	..	8 44	..	1242	..	3 40	..	..	..	7 38	..					..	..	..	..
—	25¼ Alton A .... arr	..	..	8 51	..	1249	..	3 47	..	..	..	7 46	..					..	..	..	..
79	Waterloo 76 ...... arr	8 57	9 57	10 16	1246	1254	2 17	3 46	4 46	5 17	6 46	7 16	8 16	9 16	9 46			1016	1 16	6 16	9 46

A Station for Selborne (4½ miles).   **B** Station for Hambledon (3 miles).   **S** Arr. 10 16 a.m. on Saturdays.
D Station for Twyford.   **F** Station for Bishopstoke.   **G** Southampton Terminus (for Docks).   **H** 1 mile from Winchester Chesil Station.
K Dep. 4 27 p.m. on Saturdays.   **P** Arr. 5 27 p.m.   **Y** Arr. 2 12 p.m on Saturdays.
Z Arr. 7 48 p.m.

For Brockhurst and Gosport Stations closed, served by buses operated by Gosport and Fareham Omnibus Co. Provincial Services.

LOCAL TRAINS between Knowle Halt and Fareham, see Table 75.
OTHER TRAINS between London and Southampton, see Table 45.

1954

facilities at Tisted, Privett and West Meon. Goods trains ran north to Droxford until 1962 and south to Farringdon until 1968.

The story of the experimental era at Droxford station is recounted in that section of this book. The Knowle Junction to Fareham single line remains in use today by BR for its passenger services between Portsmouth and Reading together with east-west freight services.

COMPLETE removal of farms by rail is becoming increasingly popular, and the following is a typical example of these undertakings. On May 10, the entire equipment and stock of Brockwood Park Farm, near West Meon, Hants., was moved to Stalbridge, Dorset, in two Southern Railway trains. The stock included 50 sheep and lambs, 17 milch cows, 13 heifers and calves, 3 bulls, 9 hunters, a Shetland pony and her five-days-old foal, 8 ferrets, 4 dogs, and 5 pigeons. The live-stock train ran during the night, to avoid interference with evening and morning milking times, and a passenger coach was attached to it for the accommodation of 14 farm hands. The machinery and household gear was removed during the afternoon, 19 furniture containers being loaded on the train. The only animal to miss the train was the farm cat, which had absented himself, cat-like, from the unseemly din of removal.

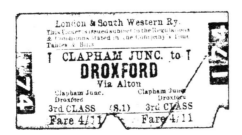

From "The Railway Magazine" of July 1933

TRAIN SERVICES

The Basingstoke and Alton Light Railway train service in its opening year was a disappointment to local residents as there were only three return journeys each day and no trains in the evening. An extra trip was added in 1903. By 1910, there were six services each way, but still none in the evenings after 8pm. After the reopening in 1924, it was back to square one with only three return journeys and the last wheel turning at 5.9pm. Public pressure brought no more trains but they were spread out over twelve hours each day instead of seven. There was no Sunday service.

The Meon Valley line was initially provided with five trains each way on weekdays (with an additional one on Saturdays) and two on Sundays. In 1910, the latter did not operate north of West Meon. By 1914 there were six weekday journeys and on Sundays, two through trains were run with one extra between Fareham and Wickham in the morning. The maximum frequency was reached prior to World War II with seven weekday and three Sunday trains. Steady decline occurred until, in 1952, Sunday trains were withdrawn and only four ran on weekdays, the last departure from Alton being at 4.30pm, of little value to business people.

THROUGH TRAINS BETWEEN

DEAL, FOLKESTONE, DOVER, MARGATE, etc.,

AND

SOUTHAMPTON, BOURNEMOUTH, etc.,

Via GUILDFORD.

From EAST to WEST —
Week Days.

	SX	SO
	a.m.	a.m.
Sandwich .. .. dep.	9 13	9 48
Deal .. .. "	9 23	9 40
Walmer .. .. "	9 28	9 28
Martin Mill .. .. "	9 35	9 35
Dover Priory .. "	9 48	9 48
Folkestone Central .. "	10 8	10 8
Shorncliffe .. "	10 11	10 11
Margate .. .. "	9h20	9m20
Broadstairs .. .. "	9h27	9m29
Dumpton Park .. "	9h31	9m33
Ramsgate .. .. "	9h36	9m38
Minster Junc. (Thanet) .. "	9h44	9 57
Canterbury West .. .. "	10h3	10 15
Ashford (Kent) .. .. "	10 33	10 40
Tonbridge .. .. "	11 8	11 20
Redhill .. .. "	11 40	11 49
	p.m.	p.m.
Guildford .. .. arr.	12 13	12 21
Guildford .. .. dep.	12 23	12 23
Ash .. .. arr.	12h48	12h48
Aldershot .. .. "	12 39	12 39
Farnham .. .. "	12 48	12 48
Alton .. .. "	1 4	1 4
Winchester .. .. "	1 37	1 41
Eastleigh .. .. "	1 48	1 52
Southampton Central .. "	2 2	2 10
Lyndhurst Road .. "	2 18	2 25
Brockenhurst .. "	2 29	2 36
Sway .. .. "	2g57	3g4
New Milton .. .. "	2 42	2 49
Hinton Admiral .. "		
(for Highcliffe-on-Sea) .. "	3g11	3g16
Christchurch .. "	2 51	2 58
Pokesdown (for Eastern Bournemouth) .. "	2 57	3 4
Boscombe .. .. "	3 0	3 7
Bournemouth {Central .. "	3 4	3 11
{West .. "	3 16	3 23

From WEST to EAST —
Week Days.

	SX	SO
	a.m.	a.m.
Bournemouth {West .. dep.	10h50	10h50
{Central	11 A 0	11 A 0
Boscombe	11 5	11 4
Pokesdown (for Eastern Bournemouth) ..		
Christchurch	11 9	11 7
Hinton Admiral	11 14	11 12
(for Highcliffe-on-Sea) ..		
New Milton	11 21	11 19
Sway	11 29	11 26
Brockenhurst	11 36	11 33
Lyndhurst Road	11 43	11 40
	11h16	11 51
Southampton Central ..	p.m.	p.m.
Eastleigh	12 4	12 4
Winchester	11w56	11w56
Alton	12 31	12 31
Farnham	1 5	1 5
Aldershot	1 21	1 21
Ash	1 29	1 29
Guildford .. arr.	1 37	1 37
Guildford .. dep.	1 47	1 47
Redhill .. arr.	2 3	1 53
Tonbridge	2 33	2 31
Ashford (Kent)	3 5	3 0
Canterbury West	3 36	3 45
Minster Junc. (Thanet) ..	4h7	4 10
Dumpton Park	4h23	4 25
Ramsgate	4h33	4 35
Broadstairs	4h40	4 42
Margate ..	4h44	4 46
Shorncliffe	4h53	4 54
Folkestone Central	3 56	5h10
Dover Priory	3 59	4 20
Martin Mill	4 13	4 34
Walmer	4 27	4 49
Deal	4 33	4 55
Sandwich	4 38	4h46
	4n49	4h38

A Seats in compartments may be reserved, 1/- per seat. Application with fee to reach Station Master before 4 p.m. day prior to the journey.
b Change at Guildford.
0 Also dep. Sandwich 9 29 a.m., changing Minster Junction (Thanet) and Guildford.
d Change at Southampton Central. **g** Change at Brockenhurst. **H** Change at Ashford.
h Change at Minster Junction (Thanet). **m** Change at Tonbridge.
n Also due Sandwich 4 38 p.m. by changing at Ashford and Minster Junction (Thanet).
SO Saturdays only. **SX** Saturdays excepted. **w** Change at Winchester.

LONDON, ALTON, DROXFORD, FAREHAM, EASTLEIGH, and SOUTHAMPTON.

Down. — Week Days / Sundays.

Mls from London	Station	mrn	mrn	mrn	mrn	mrn	mrn	mrn	aft	aft	aft	aft	aft	aft	aft	mrn	mrn	mrn	mrn	aft	aft	aft	aft
	London (Waterloo) 388 dep.	557	627	7 25	7 27	1027	1027	1127	1157	1257	227	257	427	427	657	725	..	7 25	9 27	1027	3 27	6 27	657	..
48¼	Alton............dep.	726	..	..	8 56	..	1156	**H**	1 26	..	..	426	..	556	..	856	8 23	..	..	1056	..	..	..	828
51¼	Farringdon...........	733	..	..	9 3	..	12 3	..	1 33	..	..	433	..	6 3	..	9 3	8 30	..	11 3	..	..	..	835	
52½	Tisted..............	737	..	..	9 7	..	12 7	..	1 37	..	..	437	..	6 7	..	9 7	8 35	..	11 8	..	..	..	841	
55½	Privett.............	744	..	..	9 14	..	1214	..	1 44	..	..	444	..	614	..	914	8 43	..	1115	..	..	..	848	
59½	West Meon..........	752	..	..	9 22	..	1222	..	1 52	..	..	452	..	621	..	922	8 51	..	1123	..	..	..	856	
63¾	Droxford **B**......	8 9	..	..	9 29	..	1229	..	1 59	..	..	459	..	628	..	929	9 0	..	1132	..	..	..	9 4	
68¼	Wickham............	822	..	..	9 39	..	1239	..	2 9	..	..	5 9	..	637	..	939	9 9	..	1141	..	..	..	913	
70¾	Knowle Platform.....	829	..	..	9 44	..	1244	..	2 14	..	..	514	..	643	..	944	9 15	..	..	..	..	..	919	
72¾	Fareham 374, 378 arr.	835	..	..	9 50	..	1250	..	2 20	..	..	520	..	648	..	950	9 21	924	1152	..	..	..	925	1017
76¼	Fort Brockhurst....	851	..	..	1012	..	..	..	1 10	..	2 47	..	5429	..	712	..	959	931	..	**h**	..	..	**h**	1024
77	Gosport...........arr.	855	..	..	1017	..	..	..	1 14	..	2 51	..	5426	..	716	..	103	935	..	..	..	..	..	1030
—	Alton...............	..	753	8 56	..	1156	..	..	1 4	..	2 26	356	..	556	..	826	..	9 0	..	12 54	558	15	..	
51¼	Medstead & Four Marks.	..	8 5	9 8	..	12 8	..	..	..	..	2 38	4 8	..	6 8	..	838	..	9 12	..	1217	78	27	..	
54½	Ropley.............	..	810	9 14	..	1214	..	..	..	..	2 44	414	..	614	..	844	..	9 17	..	1222	5 138	33	..	
57	Alresford...........	..	818	9 18	..	1218	..	..	..	..	2 48	418	..	618	..	848	..	9 22	..	1228	5 188	38	..	
60½	Itchen Abbas........	..	825	9 25	..	1225	..	..	..	..	3 0	425	..	625	..	855	..	9 28	..	1235	5 258	45	..	
66	Winchester **C**...arr.	..	835	9 33	..	1235	..	1137	..	..	3 14	436	..	637	..	9 6	..	9 41	..	1246	5 368	57	..	
69	Shawford **D**.......	..	853	9 44	..	1245	..	2 15	..	..	3 21	442	..	643	..	927	..	9 48	..	1253	5 539	4	..	
73	Eastleigh **F** 374, 378 "	..	9 0	9 52	..	1252	..	1-48	..	..	3 29	450	..	651	..	935	..	9 55	..	1 06	39	11	..	
75½	Swaythling........ "	..	9 9	10 c5	..	1 17	..	2 33	..	..	3 40	457	..	658	..	937	..	10c2	..	1 28	6 109	20	..	
76½	St. Denys 374...... "	..	913	10 c9	..	1 21	..	2 37	..	..	3 44	5 1	..	7 2	..	101	..	1036	..	1 326	149	24	..	
77¾	Northam........... "	..	916	10 c13	..	1 25	..	2 41	..	..	3 48	5 5	..	7 6	..	105	..	..	..	..	..	..	..	
78½	Southampton **G** 524 "	..	920	10 c17	..	1 29	..	2 45	..	..	3 52	5 9	..	710	..	109	..	1042	..	2 216	201020		..	
78½	Southampton Cen. "	..	..	10g9	..	1 18	..	2s2	..	..	510	..	713	..	..	..	..	1017	..	1 206	29	30	..	

Up. — Week Days / Sundays.

Mls	Station	mrn	mrn	mrn	mrn	mrn	mrn	**Q**	aft	aft	aft	aft	aft	aft	aft	mrn	mrn	mrn	mrn	aft	aft	aft
*	Southampton Cen. dep.	..	..	647	..	9 55	..	12 4	1246	..	152	4S20	..	648	..	..	..	1024	3 24	..	6 41	..	
*	Southampton Ter. "	615	657	..	9 40	..	1130	12 39	..	2 0	..	625	..	..	..	7 20	..	2 55	..	6 48	..	
—	Northam.......... "	618	..	7 0	..	9 43	..	1133	12 33	..	2 3	..	628	..	..	..	..	..	..	..	..	
2	St. Denys........ "	622	..	7 5	..	10 2	..	1137	12 53	..	2 7	4S28	..	635	..	..	7 25	103	0 3 30	..	6 53	..	
3	Swaythling....... "	626	..	7 9	..	9 51	..	1141	12 56	..	211	4SX31	..	638	..	..	7 29	10	c3 33	..	6 57	..	
5¼	Eastleigh **F**..... "	634	..	742	..	1018	..	1156	1 18	..	218	4 20	..	7 8	..	..	7 45	1046	3 40	..	7 4	..	
9¼	Shawford **D**...... "	642	..	749	..	1025	..	12 6	1 25	..	225	4 27	..	715	..	..	7 52	1053	3 47	..	7 12	..	
12¼	Winchester **C**..... "	650	..	757	..	1032	..	1231	1 32	..	232	4 34	..	722	..	..	7 59	11	0 3 55	..	7 20	..	
17¼	Itchen Abbas.......	7 2	..	8 9	..	1044	..	..	1 44	..	244	4 44	..	734	..	..	8 11	1112	4 7	..	7 32	..	
21¾	Alresford..........	7 9	..	816	..	1051	..	..	1 51	..	251	4 51	..	741	..	..	8 18	1119	4 14	..	7 39	..	
24	Ropley.............	713	..	824	..	1057	..	..	1 57	..	257	4 57	..	747	..	..	8 26	1125	4 20	..	7 45	..	
27¼	Medstead & Four Marks.	725	..	833	..	11 7	..	..	2 7	..	3 7	5 7	..	757	..	..	8 36	1135	4 30	..	7 55	..	
31¼	Alton **A** 390.....arr.	734	..	842	..	1117	..	1 4	2 17	..	317	5 17	..	8 7	..	..	8 45	1144	4 40	..	8 5	..	
—	Mls Gosport.....dep.	..	7 35	..	10 3	..	1110	..	..	215	351	..	..	620	..	8 13	5 5	..	..	820	..	..	
—	¼ Fort Brockhurst..	..	7 38	..	10 6	..	1113	..	..	218	354	..	..	623	..	8 16	5 8	**h**	..	623	**h**	..	**y**
—	Mls Fareham.....dep.	..	7 54	..	1017	..	1150	..	..	248	417	..	..	630	..	8 50	816	8 21	..	631	636	..	9 29
—	2 Knowle Platform...	..	7 59	..	1024	..	1154	..	..	252	422	..	..	634	..	8 54	..	8 27	..	..	642	..	
—	4½ Wickham.........	..	8 3	..	1029	..	12 0	..	..	258	429	..	..	7 0	..	9 0	..	8 33	..	..	648	..	9 37
—	9½ Droxford **B**......	..	8 12	..	1040	..	1210	..	..	3 8	440	..	..	710	..	9 10	..	8 43	..	..	658	..	9 49
—	13½ West Meon.......	..	8 21	..	1048	..	1218	..	..	317	448	..	..	719	..	9 18	..	8 52	..	..	7 7	..	9 58
—	17¼ Privett...........	..	8 30	..	1059	..	1232	..	..	329	5 2	..	..	729	..	9 32	..	9 5	..	..	718	..	10 9
—	20½ Tisted...........	..	8 36	..	11 5	..	1238	..	..	336	5 8	..	..	736	..	9 39	..	9 13	..	..	725	..	1016
—	22½ Farringdon.......	..	8 41	..	1110	..	1242	..	..	340	512	..	..	740	..	9 43	..	9 19	..	..	730	..	1021
—	25¾ Alton **A** 397...arr.	..	8 49	..	1118	..	1249	..	..	347	519	..	..	748	..	9 51	..	9 27	..	..	738	..	1029
78¾	London (Waterloo) 330 arr.	857	1016	955	1246	1246	2 16	2 146	3 46	516	649	448	6 48	916	1116	..	1116	1016	1 166	16	..	916	9 46	1218

A Station for Selborne (4½ miles).   **B** Station for Hambledon (3½ miles).   C 1 mile from Cheesefelt Station.   c 3 mins.
later Sats.   **D** Sta. for Twyford.   d 13 mins later Sats.   **F** Sta. for Bishopstoke.   **G** Southampton Terminus, for Docks.
g Arr. 10 25 mrn. commencing 5th Sept.   **H** Thro Train, Deal, Dover, & Folkestone to Bournemouth, pages 43s, 277, 274,
388, & 324a.   **h** Thro Train to or from Portsmouth and Southsea, pages 377 & 381.   i Arr. 1 41 aft. Sats.   k Arr. 5 17 aft.
on Tues, Weds, & Thurs.   i 19 mins. later on Sats.   **Q** Thro Train, Bournemouth West to Folkestone, Dover, and Deal,
via Guildford, pages 330a, 330, 277, 274, & 37.   **SX** Sats. excepted.   **y** Thro Train, Portsmouth and Southsea to Ascot, pages
381, 391, & 386.   y 6 mins later Sats.   z Arr 2 10 aft Sats.   * Miles from Southampton Terminus.   ‡ Change at Aldershot.

LOCAL TRAINS between Winchester and Southampton, page 382.—Fareham and Gosport, 374.
OTHER TRAINS between London and Southampton, page 324.—Knowle Platform and Fareham, 374.

SOUTHAMPTON, TOTTON, and FAWLEY.—Week Days only.

Mls	Station	mrn	aft	aft	8 X	aft	Mls	Station	mrn	S X	aft	aft	aft
	London (Waterloo) **K** 324 dep.	..	8 X	z2 35	3 30	3 30		Fawley (Hants)..........dep	8 6	1155	1212	5 19	6 43
	Southampton Terminus dep.	..	..	5 31	5 38		3	Hythe (Hants)...........	8 14	12 3	1228	5 27	6 51
1¾	Southampton Central. "	6 57	..	4 11	5 38	5 44	6	Marchwood............	8 25	1213	1229	5 38	7 1
2¾	Millbrook..............	7 2	..	5 42		9¼	Totton **L** 324	8 37	1225	1241	5 51	7 13
4½	Redbridge.............	7 7	..	5 48		10¼	Redbridge 378..........	8 40	..	1243	5 54	7 15
5	Totton **L**.............	7 10	..	4 2	4 19	5 51	12	Millbrook.......(524)	8 44	..	1247	6 0	7 20
8½	Marchwood............	7 22	..	4 11	4 29	6 2	12¼	Southampton Cen. 330, arr.	8 48	..	1251	6 4	7 24
11¾	Hythe (Hants).........	7 33	..	4 21	4 39	6 12	14¼	Southampton **G** 524.. "	8 55	..	..	..	7 31
14¼	Fawley (Hants)....arr.	7 43	..	4 31	4 49	6 22	94	London (Waterloo) **K** 330 arr.	1030	..	2 39	8 15	10y39

G Southampton Terminus (for Docks).   **K** Via Southampton Central.   **L** Station for Eling.
8 X or **SX** Saturdays excepted.   **Y** Arr. 10 23 aft. on Sats. until 3rd Sept.
LOCAL TRAINS between Southampton and Redbridge, see page 382.
OTHER TRAINS between Southampton and Totton, see page 324.

The Meon Valley saw some through trains between Gosport and Waterloo in the early years. Through running from Gosport (and sometimes Portsmouth) of a few trains was always a feature of the timetable but extension north of Alton was infrequent after electrification. For example, the last up evening train on Sundays commenced at Portsmouth and for many years ran through to Ascot and, in later years, to Woking.

Mid-Hants line services in 1869 consisted of four trains each way between Waterloo and Southampton, reversing at Guildford and calling at all stations south thereof. By 1890, there were six services on weekdays and two on Sundays, all taking the later more direct route from Farnham to London. A similar service was operating when the Southern Railway came into existence in 1923. A weekday timetable of seven stopping trains was provided in 1938 together with a non-stop journey between Alton and Winchester, part of a through service between the Kent coast and Bournemouth. The Sunday timetable provided four trains, an arrangement that still prevailed in 1957. Post-war weekday services were of 9 or 10 trains until the introduction of the diesel-electric multiple units in November 1957. This brought about the best service ever – sixteen trains daily (one less on Sundays) with an extra evening trip from Alton to Alresford, on Mondays to Fridays. The latter was withdrawn in January 1967.

Basingstoke towards Alton

BASINGSTOKE

1. The first station was opened on 10th June 1839, at the same time that the line from Winchester to Southampton Terminus was brought into use. The Basingstoke to Winchester link came into use on 11th May 1840. Stationmaster Barnes is seen here in 1898, displaying his gold chain. The posters are worthy of close study. (D. Cullum Coll.)

3. The present station buildings were erected in 1903. Being a little further south than its predecessor, seen on the left, it was possible to provide four through platforms for LSWR trains as quadrupling of the tracks from London was completed about this time. (D. Cullum Coll.)

2. In the distance a train from Waterloo can be seen entering the station whilst in the foreground the horse being led along the up line is more likely to have been the local motive power for wagon shunting than a runaway. The period costumes and the fine balanced canopy brackets deserve careful examination. (D. Cullum Coll.)

4. Adams class X6 4–4–0 no. 658 leaves for Waterloo, passing under a gantry of pneumatically operated signals. On the right of the fence can be seen the separate terminal buildings of the GWR branch from Reading. (Lens of Sutton)

5. A westbound train, hauled by class T3 4–4–0 no. 574 standing on the bridge spanning the road under the platforms. The bay platform on the right was usually the starting point for the branch line trains to Alton. (Lens of Sutton)

6. The Alton branch turned southwards from the main line about half a mile west of Basingstoke station, just before the Park Prewett Hospital branch turned off northwards. There followed sidings from Thornyrofts Lorry Works (illustrated here) which were both sides of the line and also a siding for the Shell Mex and BP Brook Street Depot. Traffic on this part of the branch ceased in 1967. (A.E. Bennett)

Miles.	BASINGSTOKE, HERRIARD, and ALTON.—London and South Western.								Miles.									
	Week Days.									**Week Days.**								
	Waterloo Station,	mrn	mrn	mrn	aft	aft	aft			Waterloo Station,	mrn	mrn	mrn	aft	aft	aft		
	150 London ....dep.	5 50	7 40	11 15	12 50	2 50	5 0	....		136 London ....dep.	6 0	8 55	11 45	1 10	3 55	30	....	
—	Basingstoke ....dep.	7 15	9 35	12 40	2 36	4 20	6 10	....	—	Alton ....dep.	8 7	10 39	1 36	3 27	5 13	7 9	....	
3	Cliddesden	7 24	9 44	12 49	2 44	4 29	6 19	....	5	Bentworth and Lasham ...	8 22	10 54	1 51	3 42	5 28	7 24	....	
6¼	Herriard.................	7 35	9 55	1 02	5 54	4 0	6 30	....	7¾	Herriard.................	8 31	11 32	03	51	5 37	33	....	
9¾	Bentworth and Lasham ..	7 44	10 41	9 3	4 4	4 9	6 39	....	11¼	Cliddesden [126,149,152	8 42	11 42	11	25	48	7 44	....	
14¾	Alton 136, 137, 167.. arr.	8 0	10 20	1 25	3 20	5	5 6 55	....	14¾	Basingstoke 44, 120, arr.	8 52	11 24	2 21	4 12	5 58	7 54	....	
61¼	137 London (Waterloo) arr.	10 21	12 12	3 7	5 32	7	18 46	....	62¼	152 London (Waterloo) arr.	10 11	12 36	5 7	5 39	7 31	10 5	....	

Bradshaw 1910

CLIDDESDEN

7. The stationmaster with frock coat and two-tone beard also appears in the next photograph. He is posed here with his staff of one porter and one platelayer, together with assorted local children. The basic corrugated iron station building was typical of light railways. An entire railway so equipped is illustrated in our *Branch Line to Selsey*. This station became the fictional *Buggleskelly* in 1937, for the film *Oh! Mr. Porter*. (Lens of Sutton)

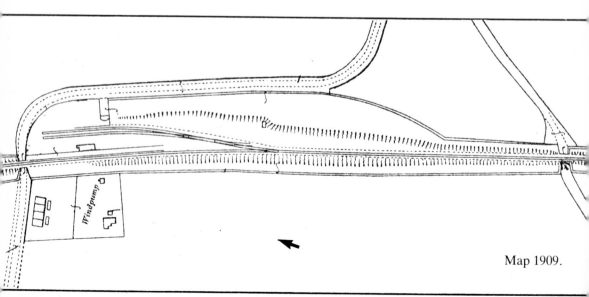

Map 1909.

8. The boiler was at the far end of this steam railcar, one of a number introduced to effect economy of operation on lightly used branch lines. Their disadvantages were noise, vibration, dirt and their limited ability to haul extra coaches or wagons. Notice the station name picked out in pieces of chalk in the grass. (P. Pickford Coll.)

1st JUNE to 30th SEPTEMBER, 1909, or until further notice.

REGULATION OF RAILWAYS ACT OF 1889.

MIXED TRAINS.

Mixed Trains, *i.e.*, Trains which convey both Passenger and Goods can only be run to the following conditions :—

(a) That the Engine, Tender and Passenger Vehicles be provided with the Vacuum Automatic Brake, worked from the Engine.

(b) That the Goods Wagons shall be conveyed behind the Passenger Vehicles, with Van or Brake Vans in the proportion of one Brake Van for every ten Wagons or fractional part of ten Wagons.

(c) That the total number of Vehicles of all descriptions on any such Mixed Train shall not exceed 25.

(d) That the maximum average speed of any such Train throughout the journey between Stations shall not exceed 25 miles an hour.

(e) That all such Trains shall stop at all Stations, or at intervals not exceeding 10 miles, or in case of Stations more than 10 miles apart, at each of such Stations.

HERRIARD

9. Prior to the railway's first closure in 1916 this station was provided with a passing loop. At each intermediate station the railway company had to dig deep wells and install pumps (wind or oil) to obtain a water supply for the station and adjacent staff cottages. The storage tank is visible in the distance. (Lens of Sutton)

Map 1910.

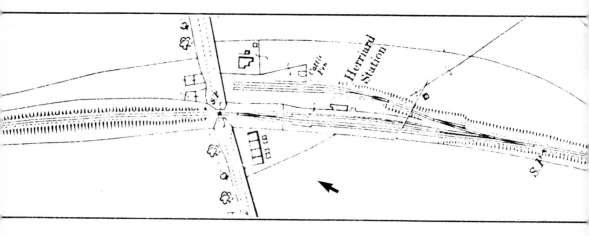

10. A train from Alton drifts into the only platform remaining in use, on 13th June 1931. The locomotive is no. 234, one of the 02 class 0–4–4 tanks, so popular on the Isle of Wight. (H.C. Casserley)

11. After re-opening, each station was provided with a staff of one, working a single shift only. The churns remind us that milk was an important traffic on the line and for this station in particular. Notice the sign *You may telephone from here*. Date – 13th June 1931. (H.C. Casserley)

12. On Sunday, 19th August 1928, a film company staged an accident for the film *The Wrecker*. A set of condemned SECR coaches and a class F1 locomotive no. A148 were set in motion downhill to collide with a Foden steam lorry. For added effect, the track had been undermined to ensure a derailment and the lorry had been filled with five tons of ballast and a charge of dynamite for good measure. (R.C. Riley Coll.)

Instructions to District Superintendents, Station Masters, Inspectors, Enginemen, Guards, Signalmen, and all others concerned, as to the

OPENING OF THE
BASINGSTOKE AND ALTON LIGHT RAILWAY
On SATURDAY, JUNE 1st, 1901,

FOR

PASSENGERS, PARCELS AND GOODS TRAFFIC.

A New Single Line, 12 miles 72 chains in length, has been constructed between Basingstoke "C" Box and Butt's Junction Signal Box. The gauge of this New Line is 4 feet 8½ inches. No Engine, Carriage, or Truck bringing a greater weight than fourteen tons upon the rails by any one pair of wheels must be run on this Railway.

The speed of Trains must not exceed 20 miles per hour at any time, or 10 miles per hour when passing over any curve the radius of which shall be less than nine chains.

For the present, Trains to and from the Alton Light Railway will travel between Basingstoke Station Down Bay Road and the "C" Signal Box on the Siding, next to the Down Main Line.

There are three intermediate Stations, viz. :—Cliddesden, Herriard and Bentworth and Lasham.

The Line will be worked under Tyer's Train Tablet System (No. 6 Instruments) as described in Instruction No. 17, 1898, which has been supplied to all concerned.

13. The solid tyres, drive chain and sprocket of the steam waggon (Fodens always used "gg" in their spelling!) are in the foreground. Actors then entered the wrecked coaches (no doubt with suitable bottles of tomato sauce) and were "rescued" during the day. (R.C. Riley Coll.)

1st JUNE to 30th SEPTEMBER, 1909, or until further notice.

PERMANENT SPEED RESTRICTIONS
THE UNDERMENTIONED SPEED RESTRICTIONS MUST BE STRICTLY ADHERED TO.

Down Trains. Maximum speed per hour.	Points at or between which speed must be reduced.	Up Trains. Maximum speed per hour.
	BASINGSTOKE AND ALTON LINE.	
10	When passing over curves between 57½ and 58½ mile posts, between Lasham and Butt's Junction	10
10	When approaching and within 300 yards of the following Crossings :—	10

Name of Crossing.	Distance from London via Basingstoke.	Stations between
Viables	49¾	Basingstoke and Cliddesden.
Bushey Warren	53½	Cliddesden and Herriard.
Grange Road ...	53¾	Cliddesden and Herriard.
Herriard Common	55	Herriard and Lasham.
Salter Ratch ...	55¾	Herriard and Lasham.

Down Trains		Up Trains
25	Over other portions of the Line	25

14. None of the three intermediate stations served more than four hundred local inhabitants, the chalk uplands being thinly populated due to lack of natural water supplies. This remote station is seen with early style nameboard and original lattice fencing, beyond which one cattle truck and an open wagon can be seen. Sliding doors were unusual for a station. (Lens of Sutton)

London and South Western Ry.
787
FROM WATERLOO TO
BENTWORTH & LASHAM

16. When photographed in September 1983, the station site was used by a coal merchant and the station building was still standing, after over 80 years service. When the nearby airfield was constructed, the main road was diverted along the former railway track, north west of this point. (V. Mitchell)

15. Mixed trains (i.e. passenger and goods vehicles) were permitted by the Board of Trade on Light Railways. Here we see the tail end of one such train on 23rd June 1928. Notice also the later style name board and fencing. A Great Central Railway van stands in the yard, five years after the company ceased to exist. (Late E. Wallis)

17. To the east of the junction of the three branch lines to Alton, a hospital consisting of huts was built for the treatment of survivors from the Boer War. In 1908, it became the Lord Mayor Treloar Cripples Hospital and College, the LSWR agreeing to a private siding being laid and a platform being erected. (R.W. Small Coll.)

London and South Western Ry.
787
TO
BASINGSTOKE

18. The siding was mainly used for the delivery of about 1500 tons of coal per annum and was unsuitable for locomotives. It was worked by a rope which could be put round the capstan (on the left of this April 1953 picture) and then attached to the shunting engine. Special passenger trains ran to the platform long after scheduled services ceased and coal trains ran until November 1967. (D. Cullum)

BASINGSTOKE & ALTON LIGHT RAILWAY.

WEEK DAYS ONLY.

		a.m.	a.m.	a.m	p.m.	p.m.	p.m
ONDON (Waterloo)	dep.	5 50	7 40	11 15	1250	2 45	5 0
oking	,,	6 30	8 37	11x37	1 38	3 30	5 36
ASINGSTOKE	arr.	7 19	9 24	12 20	2 28	3 59	6 7
ALISBURY	dep.	...	7 34	1023	1238	2 20	4 12
ndover Junction	,,	...	8 8	1140	1 12	2 47	4 40
ASINGSTOKE	arr.	...	8 51	11A42	1 54	3 25	5 5
BASINGSTOKE	dep.	7 11	9 35	1240	2 35	4 20	6 10
Cliddesden	arr.	7 20	9 44	12 49	2 44	4 29	6 19
Herriard	,,	7 31	9 55	1 0	2 55	4 40	6 30
Bentworth and Lasham	,,	7 40	10 4	1 9	3 4	4 49	6 39
ALTON	,,	7 56	10 23	1 25	3 20	5 6	6 55
LTON	dep.	8 39	10 30	1 32	3 35	5 33	6 59
arnham	arr.	8 56	10 46	1 48	3 51	5 50	7 15
ldershot	,,	9 6	10 56	1 59	4 1	5 59	7 24
oking	,,	9 33	11 22	3B13	4 29	6 25	7 48
ONDON (Waterloo)	,,	1013	1213	3 7	5 34	7 6	8 48
LTON	dep.	8 49	1147	3 55	2	...	7 2
inchester	arr.	9 37	12 31	3 52	5 52	...	7 45
OUTHAMPTON TOWN (for Docks)	,,	1016	1 44	27	6 27	...	8 20

		a.m.	a.m.	a.m.	p.m.		p.m.	p.m.
SOUTHAMPTON TOWN (for Docks.)	dep.	...	8 56	1159	...		1 58	3 50
Winchester	,,	...	9 35	12 41	...		2 38	4 35
ALTON	arr.	...	10 27	1 29	...		3 32	5 29
LONDON (Waterloo)	dep.	6 0	8 55	1145	1 5	1c 10	3 5	5 30
Woking	,,	6 46	9 44	12 30	2 1	2c 0	3 56	6 6
Aldershot	,,	7 15	10 11	1 0	2 33	2c32	4 29	6 32
Farnham	,,	7 24	10 18	1 9	2 43	2c43	4 39	6 41
ALTON	arr.	7 42	10 35	1 26	3 1	3 1	4 58	6 58
ALTON	dep.	8 5	10 40	1 36	3 27		5 13	7 11
Bentworth and Lasham	arr.	8 20	10 55	1 51	3 42		5 28	7 26
Herriard	,,	8 29	11 4	2 0	3 51		5 37	7 35
Cliddesden	,,	8 40	11 15	2 11	4 2		5 48	7 46
BASINGSTOKE	arr.	8 50	11 25	2 21	4 12		5 58	7 56
BASINGSTOKE	dep.	10 8	12 23	3 19	5 37	6 15	19 44
Andover Junction	arr.	10 37	12 46	3 57	6 15	6 53	7 24 10 22
SALISBURY	,,	11 2	1 18	4 32	6 54	...	7 51 11 0
BASINGSTOKE	dep.	8 59	11 31	3 20	4 22	6 29	9 6
Woking	,,	10H 0	12 034	4 0	4 56	7F7	9E46
LONDON (Waterloo)	,,	10 11	12 305	7	5 39	7 31	10 5

During June leave Salisbury10 40, Andover June. 11.24 a.m. and arrive Basingstoke 12.8 p.m. B Change at Brookwood C Saturdays only. D During e leave Basingstoke 12 12 p.m and arrive Woking 1.0 p.m. E Leave Basingstoke 9.18 p.m. F Leave Basingstoke 6.38 p.m. H Leave Basingstoke 9.17 a.m. J Saturdays excepted. K Arrive Basingstoke 12.10 p.m.

Fareham towards Alton

FAREHAM

1907 map – 6" to the mile.

19. Originally a small intermediate station on a branch line to Gosport, this station eventually became an important junction of five routes. The modest station buildings are dwarfed by the later three-storey Railway Hotel. (D. Tillman Coll.)

20. Another early postcard, showing the south end of the station and the Portsmouth lines curving away on the right. Notice the profusion of enamel advertisement signs on the parapets of the road bridge. (Lens of Sutton)

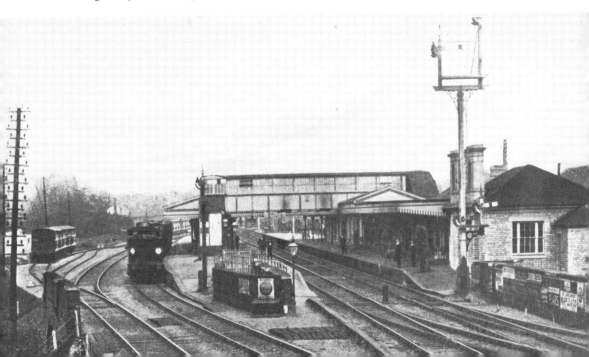

21. Looking north-west from the up bay starting signal on 19th July 1928, we see the Southampton lines turning to the left and beyond them the Fareham tunnels avoiding lines. Running straight into the distance is the original route to Eastleigh, through the tunnels. Note the variety of wagon owners and that not one of them is native SR. (Late E. Wallis)

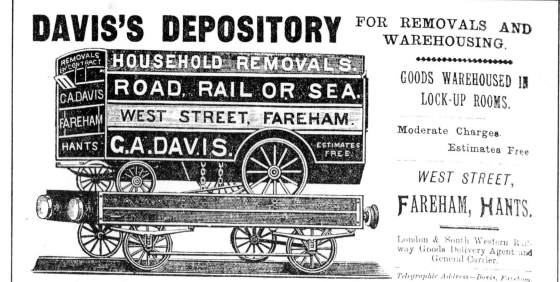

22. Class M7 no. 45 with the 6.50pm to Alton on the 10th April 1948 standing in the up bay platform. In the background is the spacious goods shed which remained in use until 1970. The goods yard is now only used for unloading road stone. (J.H. Aston)

23. A Meon Valley branch train passing Fareham East signal box on 24th June 1950. The description *East* was doubly confusing as it was to the west of *West Box* but at the *north* end of the station. The explanation was that as London was at the east end of the LSWR, the signal boxes at the London end of stations were described as *East Box*. (Pamlin Prints)

24. View of Fareham tunnels taken from a branch train in May 1953 clearly showing daylight beyond the first tunnel, only 56 yds long. The explanation for the existence of the gap is given in the introduction to this book. (P. Hay)

Diagrams illustrating the various changes in track use north of Fareham are reproduced from *The Railways of Southern England: Secondary and Branch Lines* by courtesy of the author, Dr. Edwin Course.

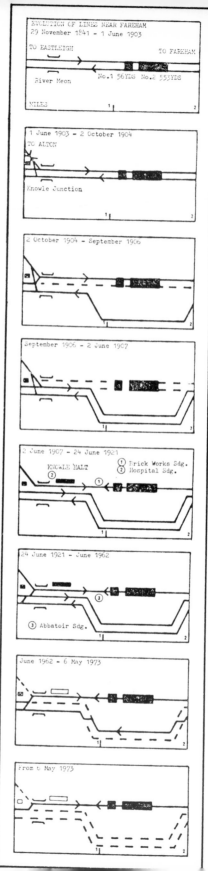

25. Fontley Brickworks siding, photo-graphed in January 1955, was a little to the north of Fareham tunnels and was closed in December 1962. Further north, but on the east side of the single line, was another private siding. This was for Fontley Abbatoir and was in use from 1953 until 1970. (D. Cullum)

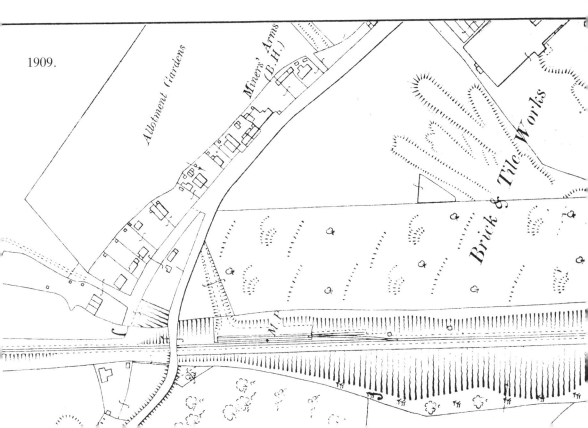

1909.

KNOWLE HALT

26. On 1st May 1907, Knowle Asylum Halt and two private sidings were opened. This view shows the former gas works in the distance and U class no. 31626 shunting at the sidings on 28th August 1961, the year before they were closed. (R.A. Holder)

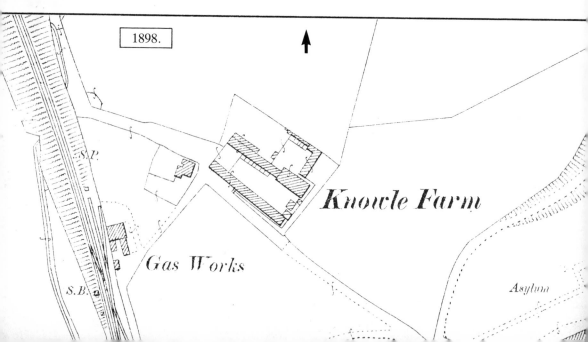

1898.

S.P.

S.B.

Gas Works

Knowle Farm

Asylum

27. The word *Asylum* was dropped in 1942. This photograph of the electrically lit halt was taken 2 months before its closure on 6th April 1964. Many trains only stopped there on Thursdays, as this was the visiting day. (E. Wilmshurst)

28. Looking north in July 1927, from the bridge over the River Meon, we see the Meon Valley line curving to the right. Knowle Junction signal box was closed on 6th May 1973, having seen more changes of track layout than most boxes in its 70 year career. (Late E. Wallis)

WICKHAM

29. The River Meon was crossed by the railway engineers just south of the station by means of a lattice steel bridge on columns. In the foreground is their Fowler traction engine (an early type with a steam dome) and a temporary timber trestle bridge. Behind it can be seen the headgear of the hoist for the columns, also probably used for pile driving. (SW Circle Archives)

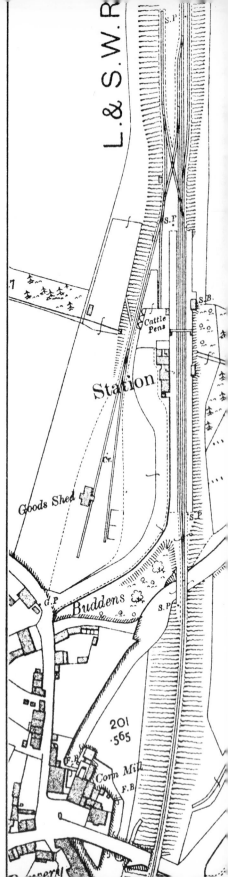

30. Driver Hickmott waits for departure time on 17th April 1954, with the Alton to Portsmouth freight. The T9 has had some clamps added to the smokebox door to maintain vacuum. (L. Elsey)

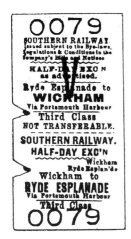

31. The inhabitants of the old country town of Wickham must have been pleased with their new railway station – not only its proximity to the town but for its architectural style. Bold gables and dormers are obvious – stone inserts in the chimneys are less so. Photographed in 1954, the buildings later suffered extreme vandalism until demolished in 1971. (A.W. Burges)

London and South Western Ry.
787
TO
WICKHAM

33. The 63-ton U class 2–6–0 locomotives were mainly used on the freight services during the final years of the branch, this one being photographed on 27th April 1962. The down siding, down loop, up headshunt and the signal box were all removed in 1957, the footbridge having disappeared in 1926. (R.M. Casserley)

32. Here we witness shunting operations on 28th December 1954 being carried out by class 700 no. 30693 and obtain a good view of the track layout and north side of the station. (P. Hay)

34. Two sidings were provided about half way between Wickham and Droxford. One was for the Meon Valley Timber Co. and the other was a public siding serving the agricul-tural and horticultural communities in the Soberton and Swanmore areas. Here we see the down goods passing the sidings on 25th April 1962. (R.A. Holder)

1910.

	ALTON, WEST MEON, and FAREHAM.—London and South Western.																		
Miles	**Down.**		**Week Days.**						**Sundays.**		Miles	**Up.**		**Week Days.**					**Sundays.**	
		mrn	mrn	mrn	aft	aft	aft		mrn	aft			mrn	mrn	aft	aft	aft	aft	mrn	aft
—	136 London .....dep.	7 10	9 20	9 50	1 10	4 12	5 30		...	...	—	Fareham ....dep.	7 40	10 39	1 37	4 30	5 26	6 47	7 44	7 11
—	Alton ....dep.	8 58	11 10	12 0	3 9	5 46	7 4		...	...	2	Knowle Platform.....		10 44				6 52		
5¼	Tisted §§	9 8	11 20	12 10	3 19	5 56	7 14		...	...	4¼	Wickham	7 49	10 49	1 46	4 39	5 35	6 57	7 53	7 20
8¾	Privett	9 15	11 30	12 17	3 26	6 3	7 21		...	...	9½	Droxford ††	7 59	10 59	1 56	4 49	5 45	7 7	8 3	7 30
12¾	West Meon........	9 22	11 37	12 24	3 33	6 10	7 32		8 20	7 45	13¾	West Meon	8 7	11 7	2 4	4 58	5 53	7 15	8 10	7 37
16½	Droxford ††	9 29	11 44	12 31	3 40	6 17	7 39		8 27	7 51	17¾	Privett	8 17	11 17	2 14	5 8	6 5	7 25		
21¾	Wickham	9 37	11 52	12 39	3 48	6 25	7 47		8 34	7 59	20¾	Tisted §§	8 23	11 23	2 20	5 14	6 11	7 31		
23¾	Knowle Platform....	9 43		1244							25¾	Alton 137, 157.... arr.	8 31	11 31	2 28	5 22	6 19	7 39		
25¾	Fareham 140, 142 arr.	9 48	12 1	12 49	3 57	6 34	7 56		8 44	8 ...	72¾	137 London (W'loo) arr.	102 11	0 4	137	1	8 46	9 29		

†† Station for Hambledon (3 miles); §§ for Selborne (2¾ miles).

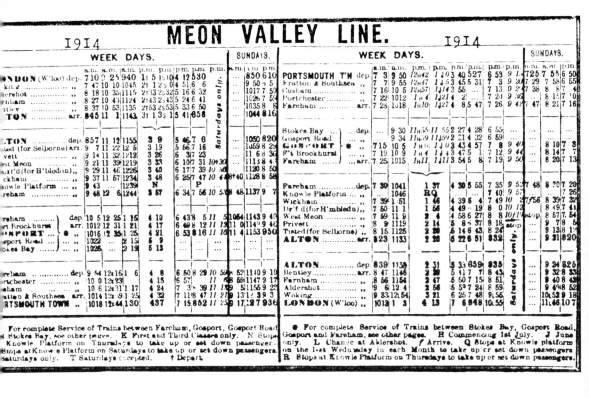

35. Mislingford (Goods) Signal Box was really a covered ground frame. No. 30693, one of the 700 class, propels its train under the loading gauge on an overcast December day in 1954. (P. Hay)

36. During World War II all stations had their nameboards removed, as they were thought to carry potentially useful information to low flying enemy airmen, escaped prisoners, travelling spies and the like. Another wartime measure was the painting of white bands on posts in pedestrian areas to assist in their location in the black-out. Bombing destroyed two of the railway cottages but eventual fame arrived when the LMS Royal Train of six coaches was shunted into the goods yard on Thursday 2nd June 1944 in preparation for a two day conference of Heads of State and Defence Chiefs to make the final plans for the invasion of Europe. (C. Campbell Coll.)

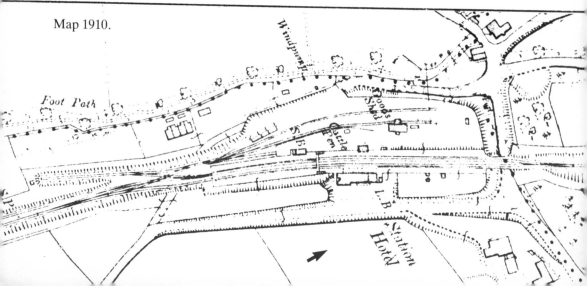

Map 1910.

37. The main buildings were on the down side and survive today, complete with the platform canopy. The train is an enthusiasts special using auto-set no. 6 in March 1959, more than four years after regular passenger services ceased. Until 1914, there were special trains for Droxford Races. (D. Fereday Glenn)

38. The goods yard had two long sidings, a cattle dock, a 5-ton capacity crane, a goods shed and a head shunt. An ageing T9 is seen leaving the yard on 28th December 1954 whilst another photographer takes a closer shot of the up platform shelter and the 24 lever signal box. (P. Hay)

39. After the thrice-weekly freight service ceased on 30th April 1962, Mr. Charles Ashby leased the branch for experiments with his 50-seat Sadler Rail Coach and new freight handling systems. Plans were made for the coach to be used on the Newport-Cowes line but vandals destroyed it by fire before this could happen. The vehicle weighed 6 tons, was powered by a 6 litre diesel engine and ran on rubber wheels with metal flanges. Stock belonging to the Southern Locomotive Preservation Society resided here until transferred to Liss on 30th May 1970. This included USA 0–6–0T no. 30064, now operating on the Bluebell Railway. (J.A.M. Vaughan)

ALTON, WEST MEON, and FAREHAM.—Southern.

1924.

† Waterloo Station. †† Station for Hambledon (3 miles). §§ Station for Selborne (2½ miles).

London and South Western Ry.

787

TO

DROXFORD

40. Mr. Ashby also acquired some rolling stock from BR, including this Terrier 0–6–0T which eventually became an inn sign on Hayling Island and later had its dignity restored when presented by Whitbreads to the Isle of Wight Steam Railway. This February 1966 photograph shows that the up platform had earlier been widened and concreted for the bulk handling of sugar beet, during the freight-only era of the line. (J. Scrace)

WEST MEON

41. Looking north, we see the signal box without windows and the lamp posts without lamps. Other equipment provided before the line opened included locomotive water columns, the only ones between Alton and Fareham. (Lens of Sutton)

42. Looking south, another early post card reveals the starkness of the freshly cut chalk. The salmon pink and brown LSWR coaches were probably forming a through train from Gosport to London. (Lens of Sutton)

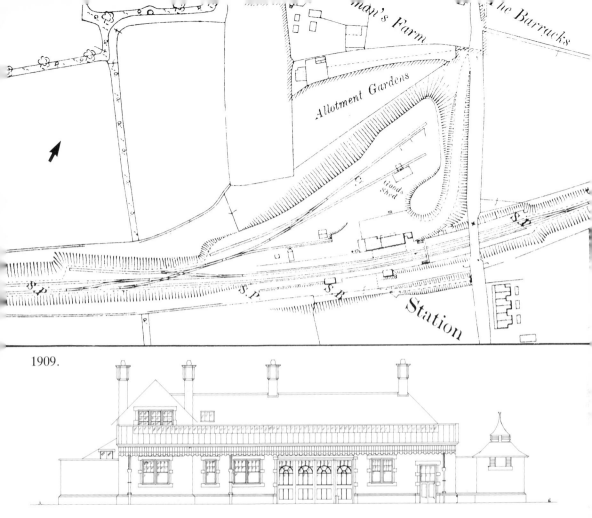

1909.

Up platform elevation. (R. Hodson)

43. A snapshot from the 1930's showing the station staff and William Stone (in shirt-sleeves) who was the local parcel agent, coal merchant and grand father of R.A. Stone, author of *The Meon Valley Railway*. (Kingfisher Press). (R.A. Stone Coll.)

44. The lavish architecture remained un-altered, when photographed a month before closure. All the intermediate stations were of a similar style and far more capacious than was required to serve the small number of local inhabitants (e.g. 2300 in 1907 in the West Meon area). Each station had a louvred pagoda-style gentlemen's toilet, seen nearest the camera. (D. Cullum)

45. The approach to, and the layout of, the goods yard was similar to that at Droxford. The foot crossing and drop in the platform edge in front of the signal box were provided when the footbridge was removed in 1926. Similar arrangements were made at Wickham and Tisted. This photograph was taken on the first day of 1955, the year of closure. (D. Cullum)

46. The River Meon was over 20 yards below rail level, on the left of the East Meon road. The four arches and their supports consumed over 700 tons of steel. (British Rail)

47. After a life of little more than 50 years, the viaduct was dismantled in 1956. The first operation was to cut holes in the decking and to shovel the ballast through them. After cutting out the steel spars to the stage illustrated, the remainder was felled, like unwanted trees. (Lens of Sutton)

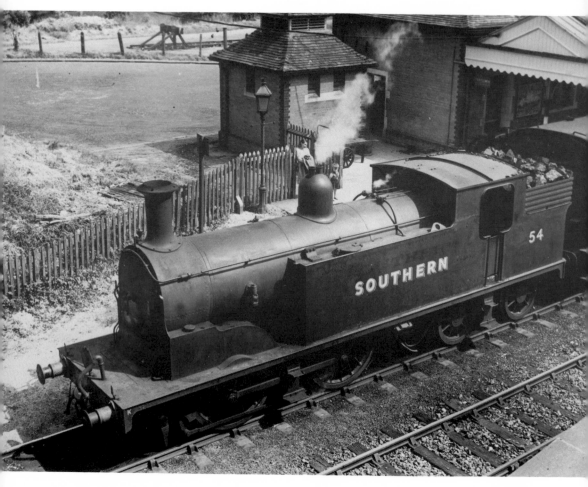

48. Another view of one of the familiar class M7 tanks showing the later style of *Southern* lettering, with the earlier style just visible above it thanks to the brilliant afternoon sunlight and chemical cleaners. Few passengers used this remote station and the absence of nearby dwellings made it a trouble free place to store restaurant and Pullman cars for the duration of World War II. Note the young locomotive admirer, by the dome. (E.C. Griffith)

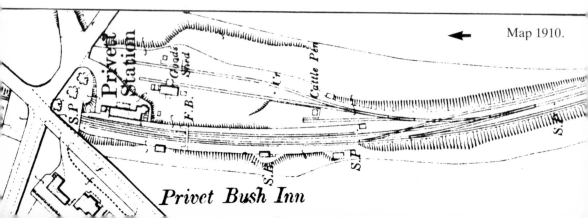

Map 1910.

49. Presentation for the best kept section of line – Butts Junction to West Meon Viaduct – taking place at Privett on 31st May 1950. Left to right: Bill Turner, Syd Jackson, Billy Goots, Harold Appleton, Len Jackson, Charlie Hunt, Wilf Pink, Mr. V.A.M. Robertson (Chief Civil Engineer), Syd Bourne, 'Chipe' Pink, Jimmy Bullen and Ern Bundy.

Harold 'Appy' Appleton retired in June 1979 after 44 years on the Railway, during which time he walked approximately 75,000 miles, equivalent to three times round the world. When he joined the Southern Railway in 1935, Harold worked as a trackman between Alresford and Winchester Junction, earning £2 5s. for a 48-hour week. He transferred to the Meon Valley Line in 1938, where he remained until its closure in 1955. (British Rail/ H. Appleton Coll.)

London and South Western Ry.

787

TO

PRIVETT

0480

SOUTHERN RAILWAY.
Issued subject to the By-Laws,
Regulations & Conditions in the
Company's Bills and Notices.

Monthly as advertised.

Privett

WEST MEON

Third Class Fare 1/2½
NOT TRANSFERABLE.

SOUTHERN RAILWAY.
MONTHLY RETURN.
West Meon
Privett

West Meon to

PRIVETT

Third Class. Fare 1/2½

0480

50. Having stood part of its train in the down platform, no. 30325 of class 700 proceeds with shunting coal wagons into the yard, on 18th December 1954. The up loop had been relegated to siding status in 1922. (S.C. Nash)

52. The summit of the line was at Privett tunnel (1058 yds. long) and heavy civil engineering was necessary for many miles each side of it. This is part of the construction gang, north of Privett. If the horse had moved suddenly, the boy was standing in an unenviable position. (R.A. Stone Coll.)

SOUTHERN RAILWAY.
Issued subject to the Bye-laws, Regulations &
Conditions in the Company's Bills and Notices.
0392   Alton to
0392
CHILD
PRIVETT
Third Class.   Fare 11½d
NOT TRANSFERABLE.

51. In 1922, the signal box was downgraded from a block post to a ground frame and was therefore unstaffed when this photograph was taken on the last day of passenger services. No. 30054 leaves for Alton on a miserable February day with the grass covered platforms and isolated setting emphasising the futility of building a station in that locality, even if it had rural charm of appeal to later railway lovers. (A.W. Burges)

TISTED

53. Looking towards Alton shortly before sunset, in the twilight years of the line, we see the familiar lavish station and spacious signal box. The track layout had originally been similar to the previous four stations but had been simplified in 1950 to the arrangement seen here. (R.C. Riley)

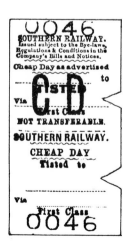

SOUTHERN RAILWAY.

(6/29)

Stock
787

TO

TISTED

54. Class M7 no. 30055 calls at "Tisted for Selborne" with an Alton train on 28th December 1954. The skew overbridge carried a minor country road. The water storage tank for the conspicuous Gents (and the rest of the station) can be seen up the hill, behind the signal box. Like Privett, the building is now a private dwelling. (P. Hay)

FARRINGDON

55. It is surprising that the residents of the village had to wait until 1st May 1931 for a passenger service when smaller places on the line had palatial stations. Another surprise is that it was called *Faringdon Platform* (spelt with only one r) between 1st May 1932 and 8th July 1934. Note the gate on the private siding to Aylwards Mill on this photograph, dated 9th August 1954. (R.M. Casserley)

Map 1910.

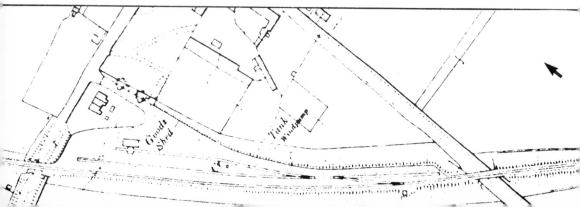

56. The down freight clanks past the wooden platform and cattle dock on 28th December 1954. The T9 class were known as Greyhounds, owing to their speedy hauling of passenger trains in their younger days. (P. Hay)

57. In the distance can be seen the ground frame controlling the entrance to the two sidings. Remarkable features include the provision of weather protection for goods wagons but none for passengers and the lack of the obligatory ramp at the near end of the platform. This shot was taken two days before the end of passenger services. (D. Cullum)

59. After removal of the passenger platform the siding was repositioned and a new concrete dock built for the handling of bulk materials, such as sugar beet. It was the last passenger station to open and it was the last goods depot to close on the Meon Valley line – 13th August 1968. Track lifting to Alton was completed by May 1970. (Lens of Sutton)

58. A further surprise was that the goods shed displayed an incorrect name, over a year after passenger trains ceased. Note the fine finials and the overcoat instead of anti-freeze for the Bedford lorry. (J.H. Aston)

Winchester towards Alton

WINCHESTER

60. The canopy and clock were amongst the later additions to Sir William Tite's original design. Now lacking doors, it was opened on 10th June 1839 for Southampton trains and in the following year, the London service commenced. This 1939 view is little changed today. (F.E. Box Coll./N.R.M.)

62. The driver of the Alton bound train on 24th June 1957 appears to have the company of the guard in his compartment. The up goods yard was mainly at right angles to the main line. A van can be seen beyond the two buffer stops on the right. It is standing on the first of three long sidings which had to be shunted by a short wheelbase locomotive such as the P and B4 class, on account of the sharp curves leading to them. The small open ended engine shed can be seen on the right of this picture. (R.C. Riley)

61. Adams class T1 no. 360 takes water on 5th April 1943 whilst passengers join its Alton-bound train. This station was named Winchester City between 1949 and 1967 to distinguish it from Winchester Chesil on the former GWR line. This was a corruption of the earlier name of Cheese Hill.
(F.E. Box Coll./N.R.M.)

63. Looking north in February 1960, we see the Mid-Hants line on the right and the former spur to the GWR on the left. After 1951 it was sometimes used for wagon storage and was eventually removed in 1962. A quarter way up the steps can be seen the platform used for handing the single line token to passing train crewmen. (E. Wilmshurst)

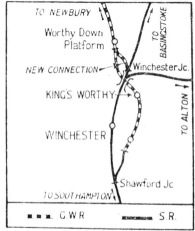

New connection near Winchester to avoid conflicting movements

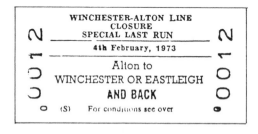

The Railway Magazine map shows as "new connection" a single line spur that was brought into use on 5th May 1943 to speed up war-time traffic between the Midlands and Southampton Docks, by avoiding the need for up trains to cross the down line at Shawford Junction.

64. This was a peaceful rural location, the signal man only being disturbed by passing trains and owls in the trees. The box closed on 25th March 1979, exactly seven years after this photograph was taken. (R. Neal)

ITCHEN ABBAS

65. The covering of ivy largely hid the ugly cement rendering on the south side of the station house, added to this elevation to reduce damp penetration of the brickwork. The avenue of beech trees added to the charm of this station approach. (Lens of Sutton)

66. The far platform and the passing loop ceased to be used on 26th September 1931 and staffing of the station ended on 6th September 1965, when conductor/guards were introduced. This train was departing for Alton on 2nd November 1957. (A.W. Burges)

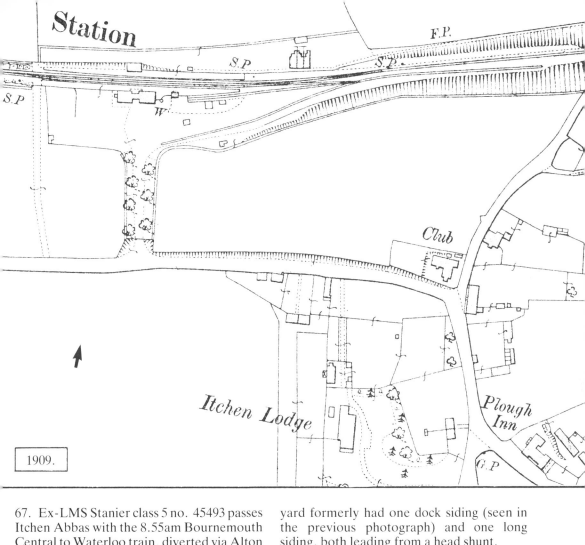

Station

F.P.

S.P.

S.P.

S.P.

W.

Club

Itchen Lodge

Plough Inn

1909.

67. Ex-LMS Stanier class 5 no. 45493 passes Itchen Abbas with the 8.55am Bournemouth Central to Waterloo train, diverted via Alton due to engineering works on the main line, on the 5th May 1966. The overgrown goods yard formerly had one dock siding (seen in the previous photograph) and one long siding, both leading from a head shunt. (J. Scrace)

ALRESFORD

68. An early postcard view of a familiar scene today, revealing how little has changed at this location. (Mid-Hants Railway Archives)

1909.

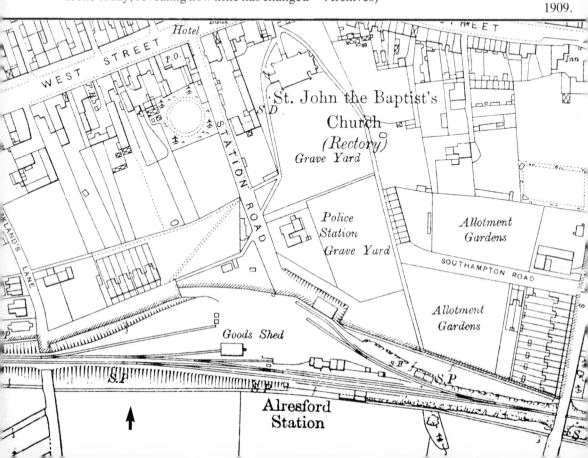

69. For nearly a century the despatch of watercress was an important activity at this station, up to 14 tons being loaded in one day in the season. Van trains would stand in the private siding close to the 1873 warehouse, now occupied by SCATS (Southern Counties Agricultural Trading Society). In the 1950s up to six vans would be required for the traffic and some would go as far as Newcastle and Glasgow. Hampshire produced more than double the tonnage of watercress of any other county and the Alresford district produced a third of that. The coming of the railway boosted the industry and about 40 acres of beds produced up to 12 tons of cress per acre each year for transport by rail. (Mid-Hants Railway Archives)

70. An undated photograph of an unwelcome vehicle in the station approach road. We have found no details of the cause of this accident. (Mid-Hants Railway Archives)

71. The story behind this picture was retold
in Mid-Hants News no. 22. ⟶
(Mid-Hants Railway Archives)

72. Class T9 no. 307 derailed just outside Alresford whilst working a down train. A steam crane was required to re-rail it. The driver of the 9.03 am Waterloo to Portsmouth & Southsea train (on 22nd April 1936) was reprimanded for passing an adverse signal. (R.W. Small Coll.)

Leading Goods Porter — Duty Sheet.
Alresford Station. 1949.

Hours 9 am to 6 pm, Lunch 12 to 1 pm, Mons. to Fri., 8.15 am to 12.15 pm Sats.

Compile daily and weekly wagon stock and counter returns. Order wagons as required. Attend yard traffic, prepare yard for shunting. Ldg.Pb.Sig. assist closing doors. Shunting duties with 9.20 am Alton and 12.12 pm Eastleigh. Store traffic for Shepparts store. Keep record of traffic in and out. Record inwards and outwards wagons, in coal and stage (?) books, obtain traders' signatures. Daily advice to traders of Goods and Coal received. Take up N.T.H. and U/E. Coil ropes and fold sheets, clean Goods shed daily. Keep yard clean. Attend loading outwards traffic, check with consignment notes, rope and sheet as necessary. Particular attention to safe loading Gush and Dent steel traffic. Assist with loading watercress traffic as able. Attach Cress van 2.50 pm freight and form 6.52 pm parcel train. Compile register of consignment notes and forward to Basingstoke. Insure (sic) all necessary wagon doors are closed and sheets in place. Lock Shed and stores at close of work.

73. Station staff at Alresford pose for an official photograph on the up platform, about 1947. Maybe their names will be forthcoming by the time this book needs reprinting.
(D. Ford Coll./Mid-Hants Railway Archives)

Winter on the Mid-Hants —50 years ago

By John Adams

All along the Mid-Hants Railway, at Itchen Abbas, Alresford, Ropley and Four Marks, Christmas morning of 1927 dawned with light rain and mild temperatures. The Christmas card holiday seemed very far away. But those who were fortunate enough to possess a 'wireless' set heard that the rain had turned to snow in the Thames Valley. By six o'clock it was snowing in North Hampshire, and by 10 o'clock on Christmas night the snow was general over all Southern England. Thus the stage was set at Alresford, for the first time in living memory, to be cut off from the outside world by road and rail.

By late evening, reports came in that trains were operating with great difficulty on the Mid-Hants and Meon Valley lines owing to deep snowdrifts: the Basingstoke—Overton and Didcot—Winchester lines were closed completely. No letters or parcels were despatched on Boxing Day, Monday, Tuesday or Wednesday. On Boxing Day morning 70 gangers were sent westwards from Alton to attempt to clear the cuttings. The "esteemed (Alresford) Station Master, Mr. Newnham", (to quote the *Hampshire Chronicle*), "did his utmost, working in fact like a Trojan, to see that the gang carried out their thankless task with as much comfort as possible, and arranged with Messrs. Batchelor and Andrews to cater for them".

On the 26th (Boxing Day), a down train had managed to get as far as Alresford but could get no further. Two up trains due away from Alresford on the same day were in great difficulties; one managing to get through to London, but the driver of the second detached his engine and in that way got through to Alton. On the 28th, a steam plough got as far as Alresford, and then worked towards Itchen Abbas in an attempt to free a train trapped in the cutting west of Alresford Station. By Thursday 29th, the line was clear on the Ropley side of Alresford. Many drifts on this section were up to 35 feet deep.

Operations were witnessed by many people assembled along the tops of the cuttings, and as one spectator so aptly said, "This is something new for England." On Thursday the first mail came through, and a shuttle service between Alresford and Alton also commenced that same day. By the morning of Friday 30th the rails between Alresford and Winchester had been cleared, but owing to the high banks of snow, the line was not judged safe for traffic. Services were not, in fact, resumed until Monday, 2nd January, 1928.

Thus ended the worst week in the history of our line, and one which many still living nearby will never forget.

74. On 15th June 1957, the up passenger train is propelled into the platform by class M7 no. 30480. On a dry summer day, the fire buckets on the fence might well be required for sleepers set alight by small coals falling from the ash pan. The down goods train can be seen better in the next picture. (A.W. Burges)

Up platform elevation. (M. Papps)

76. By the time this photograph was taken in May 1967, the siding beyond the signal had been pulled up and fares from passengers travelling from the other intermediate stations were collected by the guard – hence the satchel.. Note the old style flat top caps and the signal box name reflecting in the train windows. The leading compartment had had its seats removed to provide more space for luggage, bicycles and watercress. The latter commodity continued to be carried in small quantities by passenger trains until services ceased. (J.A.M. Vaughan)

75. One van and one 3-plank wagon was a feather-weight train for a class 700 locomotive with a tractive effort of 23,500lbs. In the last years of the line freight was worked from Woking as far as Ropley and from Eastleigh up to Alresford. The goods yard was closed in 1964. (A.W. Burges)

77. Dennis Ford lighting the gas lamps in November 1972, shortly before closure. He was one of the two regular signalmen and worked at Alresford for over 30 years. The elegant swan neck lamps on candy posts still adorn the Mid-Hants Railway.
(E.C. Griffith)

78. For six years before closure in 1973, the only passing place between Winchester Junction and Alton was at Alresford. 2H no. 1122 with an up train passes 3H no. 1128 on a down train. Note the single line token leaning against the driver's window and the shield on the gas lamp to avoid it interfering with the signalman's vision at night.
(J.A.M. Vaughan)

79. N class 2–6–0 no. 31874 arrives from Ropley with the re-opening train on 30th April 1977. The exceptionally high standard of finish of this locomotive is particularly remarkable since restoration was achieved in the open without any weather protection. (C. Small)

80. The band playing 'Congratulations' after the arrival of the re-opening train – a thought very much in everyone's mind on that memorable day. In the ensuing four years the line carried a quarter million passengers. (C. Small)

ROPLEY

81. An early view showing the signal box in the distance and a lean-to building nearest the camera. The next photograph shows that the lean-to was replaced by a two-storey extension of indifferent style. (Mid-Hants Railway Archives)

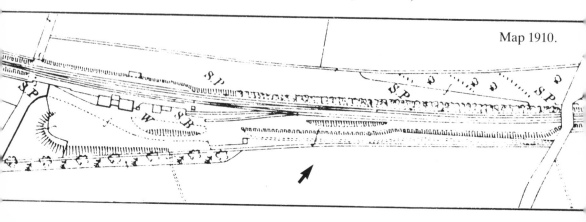

Map 1910.

82. A post card view showing the rectangular windows of the extension contrasting with the round-headed sashes of the original building. The up platform on the left, together with the loop and signal box were taken out of use in 1931. (Mid-Hants Railway Archives)

83. Topiary is described as "the art of clipping trees and shrubs into ornamental or fantastic shapes". Even the early photographs of this station show some topiary. The station became well known for this art form, the artist in later years being Walter Woodley. (Mid-Hants Railway Archives)

84. Some signs of modernisation by the Southern Railway are the cast concrete lamp posts and loading gauge. The goods yard had one long siding running under the road bridge in the distance and two short ones returning towards the station.
(Lens of Sutton)

London and South Western Ry.
——
787
TO
ROPLEY

86. Looking south-west, the exposed location is apparent as the Eastleigh to Alton freight comes to a standstill in the platform on 2nd June 1956, whilst the ground frame is unlocked. The class 700s were built at the end of the nineteenth century and were rebuilt in the 1920s with longer smokeboxes to house the superheaters. Freight services were withdrawn in 1962. (J.H. Aston)

85. In addition to propelling Motor Set no. 1, the locomotive is pulling a van. The train is the 1.55pm Eastleigh to Alton, on 9th May 1956. The small shed at the end of the platform was the lamp room where oil was once stored for the station lights and signal lamps. Lamp rooms also usually housed a rusty blunt pair of scissors for wick trimming. (J.H. Aston)

87. The south elevation (seen here in 1957) and the west end of the extension were rendered with cement to reduce water penetration. The lean-to porch on the station master's house was also a defence against the south-westerly storms. The station became unstaffed in January 1967. (A.W. Burges)

88. Maunsells class S15 no. 30837 and class U no. 31639 pass Ropley on a snowy January day in 1966 with an LCGB Rail Tour. (J. Scrace)

89. Detonators herald the arrival of rolling stock for the Mid-Hants Railway on 6th March 1976. This was the last BR train to Alresford and within a week of this photograph being taken tracklifting commenced between Alton and Ropley. (C. Small)

The development plan published in 1978 makes an interesting comparison with what exists today. Pay a visit and see the difference.

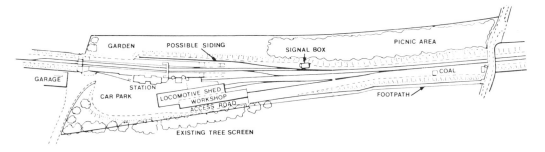

90. The first Mid-Hants Railway train arrives from Alresford, prior to testing the newly-laid track in the station and yard, on 2nd April 1977. The locomotive is the Fowler diesel shunter no. 4 and the train consists of a van, a Maunsell coach and a former GWR "Toad" brake van. (C. Small)

92. U class no. 31806 standing in front of the new engine shed which was brought into use in September 1980. The haze generated by locomotives being lit up drifts across the station on 17th April 1982. The water tower was formerly in use on the Longmoor Military Railway at Liss. (C. Small)

91. Restored to LSWR brown and cream livery, this station won the Best Preserved Station Award in 1981. Note the temporary signal cabin in the distance. Netley signal box was acquired for re-erection at the up end of the down platform. (C.R.L. Coles)

93. The Mid-Hants Railway has been used for a number of filming sequences. This photograph, taken in May 1983, shows 'Bodmin' entering Ropley with a T.V.S. 'Ultra Quiz' Special. A microphone has been clamped to the nameboard on the left. (R.W. Small)

95. Relaying the track to Medstead commenced in May 1982 at Ropley using Boyer-Schwarz track-laying gantries running on temporary 10ft. gauge rails. Secondhand track panels were brought in by road to Alresford and transported on flat bogie wagons to the railhead. The gantries, powered and propelled by small Renault engines, straddled the bogies, lifted the 60ft. long panels and moved them along into place with great precision. When photographed on 20th November, Medstead was within sight at the end of the cutting. Watching on the right is a duo of railway general managers – Greg Goodman of Mid-Hants and on his left Allan Garraway of Ffestiniog. (V. Mitchell)

94. Class 3 Diesel no. D6556 and West Country Pacific no. 34017 *Ilfracombe* double head the down *Bournemouth Belle* over Medstead Bank on 24th April 1966. The train had been diverted via Alton due to engineering works on the main line. (J. Scrace)

MEDSTEAD & FOUR MARKS

96. Opened three years after the other stations on the line, the building was of a contrasting simple design with no platform canopy. The station master's house can be seen behind the station. The exposed timber framing of the signal box was later panelled over. The name Four Marks was added on 1st October 1937 as the area had developed with smallholdings established by ex-WWI servicemen. (Lens of Sutton)

98. A small timber and corrugated iron goods shed can be seen on the extreme left of this picture, taken in the early 1950s. The oil lamps are missing – perhaps they had been removed for wick trimming and refilling. Electric lights were provided when the staff was withdrawn in 1967. (Lens of Sutton)

97. Merchant Navy class no. 35019 *French Line CGT* with the diverted 10.14am Waterloo to Bournemouth train rushes past the Winchester to Alton push-and-pull service, on the 8th May 1955. The porter/signalman appears to have been almost swept from his feet as the single line token was collected. It seems that the missing bricks of the end wall of the building were insufficient to ventilate the gentlemen's toilets as a roof ventilator was later provided. (R.C. Riley)

99. The 1965-1967 period brought a great variety of locomotives on diverted trains, much to the delight of photographers and sound recordists, some of whom can be seen on the down platform. This is the 10.34 dep- arture from Bournemouth Central hauled unaided by West Country class no. 34059 *Sir Archibald Sinclair*, now awaiting restoration on the Bluebell Railway. (J. Scrace)

101. With a hard frost covering the sleepers, no. 1133 prepares to stop at Medstead and Four Marks with a train for Southampton. Although some of the former passing loop remained in situ, it had not been used since 23rd January 1967, when the signal box also closed. Until then it had been used at 19.44, on Mondays to Fridays, to pass DEMUs. Had the rails been icy and the train slipped, the young lady on the left might not have completed crossing the track. Unlike the later Meon Valley line, the Railway Inspectorate had not demanded footbridges at the smaller stations. (J.A.M. Vaughan)

London and South Western Ry.
———
787
TO
MEDSTEAD

100. Four months later we see a down Bournemouth train double headed by nos. D6577 and 34023 *Blackmore Vale* (now active on the Bluebell Railway) having just reached the summit of the line, over 650ft. above sea level, after climbing at 1 in 60 for the 3½ miles from Butts Junction. (J. Scrace)

102. U class 2–6–0 no.31806 storms into Medstead and Four Marks on 29th May 1983 with an afternoon train during the first weekend of operation over the extension. On the right is the site of the former goods yard which had one public siding, a 3-ton crane, a cattle dock and a private siding. The latter crossed Station Approach and entered a building occupied by Hutchings, until about 1934. The yard closed in 1964. (C. Small)

103. On the same day we see the N class locomotive no.31874 piloting T9 no.30120 on a down train. In both photographs it is evident that final levelling and aligning of the track had not taken place. Nevertheless, the relaying of nearly three miles of standard gauge track in little over a year mainly by volunteers is history worth recording. (C. Small)

104. An Alton to Eastleigh train approaching Medstead and Four Marks in 'Southern' days. No. 109 was one of the class M7 tanks, so popular on the line for a large number of years. 104 were built between 1897 and 1911. The deep chalk cuttings on the line have a large angle of repose but do give rise to rock falls, particularly after frost and when the shrubs grow too heavy for their anchorage. (E.C. Griffith)

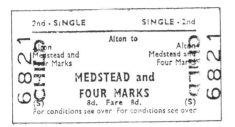

2nd - SINGLE	SINGLE - 2nd
Alton to	
6821 Alton Medstead and Four Marks	Alton Medstead and Four Marks 6821
MEDSTEAD and FOUR MARKS	
(S) 8d. Fare 8d. (S)	
For conditions see over	For conditions see over

105. A minor mishap in August 1939 when M7 class no. 49 slid on wet rails into the brake van of an engineering train. The bridge just visible in the left of the picture carried the railway over the Alton to Four Marks road. (E. Plomer)

BUTTS JUNCTION

106. Looking east on 23rd June 1928, we see the Meon Valley line on the right; the Mid-Hants line in the centre and the Basingstoke lines on the left, which converge behind the bushes. (Late E. Wallis)

107. A closer view of the signal box on the same day, showing the elevated platforms each side of the track to facilitate the transfer of the single line tokens to passing engine crews. The one on the right doubled up as a lamp room. (Late E. Wallis)

108. Following the abolition of Butts Junction in February 1935, the first floor of the original box was removed and the roof lowered for use by the Permanent Way Dept. The double track was then operated as two single lines from Alton. A ground frame controlled the siding to Treloar's Hospital until traffic ceased in 1967. (D. Cullum)

109. Maunsell Q class 0–6–0 no. 30535 passes the entrance to Courages Brewery siding, just west of Alton, on 25th October 1952. This private siding was closed on 26th November 1968. Alton has been a centre for brewing for many years and the town is still surrounded by acres of hop fields, an unusual sight outside Kent. (D. Cullum)

The map of 1896 was made at a time when Alton was just a passing place on a single line. It is clear that the goods yard did not have to be moved when the passenger lines were re-routed. Notice the wagon turntables and the locomotive turntable.

→

Alton

Workhouse

S.P

P.H

STATION ROAD

Crane

M.P

Railway
Terrace

River

Wey

S.B

S.P

Station

600 Yds.

PAPER MILL

S.P

LANE

Hopkiln
W

WINCHESTER

S.P

Prospect
Place

Alton Mills

(Paper)

Easton's
Cottages

King's Pond

110. The original terminal building of 1852, with its massive gables, can be seen on the left. After the opening of the second and present station (on the right) in 1865, its pre-decessor remained in use as the station master's house, until demolished to make way for an extension to the station car park. (R.W. Small Coll.)

111. The station staff in the late 19th century. (Hampshire County Museum Service)

112. Horse boxes were a common feature of the railway scene and were often attached to passenger trains, an integral compartment being provided for the groom. A case of rough shunting by an Adams class 0395 0–6–0 happened on the road bridge on 3rd February 1909. (R.W. Small Coll.)

113. Looking east from the up home signals on 23rd June 1928, we see the original station on the left with its more modest successor in the centre. The middle track was known as the up loop and was not signalled for starting down trains. The down platform became an island when the line was doubled from Farnham to Butts Junction in 1901. (Late E. Wallis)

114. Adams class 02 no. 221 departs with a Basingstoke train on 17th August 1929, passing the locomotive water filler which was boxed in to protect the valve from frost – now a largely forgotten problem of operating a steam railway. The building on the right was the station master's office. (H.C. Casserley)

115. When electric services from London commenced on 4th July 1937 they used platform 1, on the left. Later, a few peak hour services used platform 3. There was no conductor rail at platform 2, as this was used by the branch line trains. Taking water is class M7 no. 30051, heading the 12.5pm departure for Eastleigh on 25th October 1952. (D. Cullum)

116. The last train to traverse the Meon Valley line was this RCTS railtour on Sunday 6th February 1955, the day after the last public services operated. The train also appears in our *Branch Lines to Horsham* and *Branch Lines to Midhurst*, although hauled by locomotives other than the two class T9s (nos. 30301 and 30732) seen here. The gas lights were not electrified until 1970, 35 years after the London train services! (R.W. Small)

London and South Western Ry.
787
TO
ALTON

117. Entire farm removals by rail brought excitement and bustle for a day or two to otherwise quiet unhurried country goods yards. Here we see a local farmer's stock being loaded into ventilated fruit vans (not cattle trucks) on 24th March 1960, prior to departure to Crediton, Devon. The 5-ton capacity crane is just visible. This goods yard was closed on 6th January 1969. (British Rail)

118. A panoramic roofscape taken from the down starting signals on 4th April 1953. From left to right – the parcels office; the 1865 up buildings; the goods shed; the former workhouse; the 1865 down shelter; the 1901 down canopy and the elevated tank for locomotive water supply. The track at the London end of platform 2 was lifted in July 1967 and the siding on the right was taken out of use in April 1970. (D. Cullum)

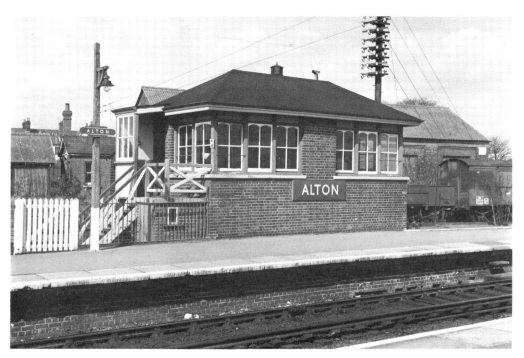

119. The 42-lever signal box, photographed here in March 1967, ceased to be used on 28th September 1980, when the track layout was simplified. Just east of the station, the electrified double track converges into a very short single line and immediately diverges into platforms 1 and 2, both points being electrically operated from Farnham. Track remains in platform 3 in readiness for Mid-Hants trains once again. (J. Scrace)

120. On 6th March 1984, the first batch of track materials for the link was transferred in BR wagons onto Mid-Hants property at Alton, opening a new chapter of railway history. (Kimroy Photos)

Books from Middleton Press

BRANCH LINE SERIES
Vic Mitchell and Keith Smith
BRANCH LINES TO MIDHURST
BRANCH LINES TO HORSHAM
BRANCH LINE TO SELSEY
BRANCH LINES TO EAST GRINSTEAD
BRANCH LINES TO ALTON
BRANCH LINE TO HAYLING
BRANCH LINE TO SOUTHWOLD

SOUTH COAST RAILWAY SERIES
Vic Mitchell and Keith Smith
BRIGHTON TO WORTHING
WORTHING TO CHICHESTER
CHICHESTER TO PORTSMOUTH

OTHER BOOKS
INDUSTRIAL RAILWAYS OF THE SOUTH-EAST
Chalk Pits Museum
GREEN ROOF OF SUSSEX
Charles Moore
MIDHURST TOWN – THEN AND NOW
Vic and Barbara Mitchell
STEAMING THROUGH KENT
STEAMING THROUGH EAST HANTS
Peter Hay
EAST GRINSTEAD – THEN & NOW
Ron Michell and David Gould